Your Secret Weapon for
Securing a Career in Law

Acknowledgements

My eternal thanks to P.B. and William, for always believing.

ISBNs:
978-1-915676-05-4 hardcover
978-1-915676-03-0 paperback
978-1-915676-04-7 ebook

Contents

i INTRODUCTION AND HOW TO USE THIS BOOK

Your CV or assessment centre has impressed recruiters and you've been invited to interview for a training contract or legal role. Congratulations! Now it's time to prepare. This book will help you get ready to really stand out at the interview stage, no matter what your background, educational achievements or experience.

Training contract interviews require a particular type of approach. These questions and sample answers have been compiled and researched over years of successfully preparing candidates for legal roles in law firms and in-house legal positions.

You can tailor each template answer to fit your own circumstances. An outline answer structure is provided for each question, some with several options so that you can choose the elements that fit best. Look out for the guidance on what the interviewer is really asking when certain questions come up, along with answers to avoid.

Being prepared is the single most important factor that determines success or failure in an interview for a legal job, or any job for that matter. The sample answers are not meant to be memorised like a script and reeled off verbatim in an interview, but you can use the ideas to prepare and practise, moulding them to fit with your own experiences, and you will have a distinct advantage over other candidates. Imagine walking into that interview knowing you already have a head-start!

These questions are designed to reflect the areas where training contract candidates often struggle, along with the things legal recruiters are looking for.

Each section is interspersed with 'Top Tips' to really help you stand out. These insights from industry recruiters, lawyers, students and successful training contract candidates cover topics such as conquering nerves, how to handle unexpected hurdles, general interview etiquette and even what to wear!

GENERAL INTERVIEW ADVICE

Any recruiter will tell you that the first thirty seconds of an interview are the deciding moments, so make your first impression count.

Arrive at reception between five and ten minutes early. Aim to get to the interview venue around 20 minutes early to allow you plenty of time to get there, find the place, park, and give yourself a few moments to mentally prepare. If you're unfortunate enough to get held up, make sure you have the interviewer's number and phone them (don't text!) to explain the delay.

When you enter the building or interview room, introduce yourself warmly and clearly, smile and make eye contact. Sit down when you're invited to, with a 'thank you'.

Shake hands only if you're comfortable doing so. A friendly smile is fine otherwise. Handshakes are becoming less common post-COVID-19 and were already falling out of expected practice before that. Some interviewers will ask, 'Are we shaking hands?' and let you decide. Don't feel that you have to say yes to be polite! If you don't like the idea, you can say so without being rude. 'That's ok, I'm happy with a hello!' said with a smile is absolutely fine. Assertiveness is a valuable asset, and how you deal with things that make you uncomfortable will be noted, so turn it into a positive. Suggesting 'Shall we elbow-bump instead?' as a compromise also shows a willingness to find common ground, hinting at the potential for good negotiating skills on your part!

Remember to relax. If you're really struggling with nervousness, turn the interview roles around in your head and imagine you're interviewing the firm to see if you want to work for them (in a sense, this is true, of course). Not only will this ease the pressure on you, it will actually be beneficial in assessing whether you'd be a good fit. Focus on how friendly the staff seem. Do they look happy? Stressed? Busy? How is the atmosphere? Does the workplace seem organised or chaotic? How do people talk to one another? Can you picture yourself working there?

The interviewer or recruiter ultimately wants to see whether they want to work with you as a person; you've already attained a certain level to even be there, so academics and experience will often come second to the first impression that you make. Throughout this book you'll find Top Tips to guide you through the interview and recruitment process. Use the sample answers to prepare your responses to the most commonly asked questions.

Good luck!

PREPARATION AND CHOOSING THE RIGHT FIT

If law students know how to do one thing, it's research. Don't submit hundreds of blanket applications to every law firm you can find. Do your homework first.

Start by thinking about factors that can help you narrow down your shortlist. Do you want to apply to big firms or small high street practices? Which areas of law do you want to work in? What about location? Once you've refined your vision of your ideal company, you can tailor your applications much more easily.

Know the company you're applying to and focus on their key areas of practice. Find out what sort of clients they undertake work for, and make sure you work these observations into your interview answers. Nothing impresses a legal recruiter more than a candidate who obviously knows a lot about the company and has a genuine interest.

Similarly, find out as much as you can about the culture of the companies you're applying to. Go to open days or law fairs and meet the staff. Do they seem happy, relaxed, passionate about the work and the firm? What sort of hours do they work? What's the office like? Is it a fast-paced environment or a smaller, boutique outfit? Ask lots of questions to get a feel for where you really want to be.

SAMPLE QUESTIONS AND ANSWERS

The first question candidates are often faced with is asked before the interview starts, and most people give the wrong answer without even realising. It may seem like innocuous, polite small talk. It may even be asked by the receptionist and not the interviewer, but your response will almost certainly be noted.

You've arrived and introduced yourself. You're waiting to be introduced to the interviewer, and someone casually asks, 'So, are you nervous?' Most candidates will smile sheepishly and say something along the lines of 'Yeah, a bit!' Turn this one around. 'Actually, I'm excited!' is an answer that will immediately set you apart from the crowd. Enthusiastic, positive and confident. A great first impression!

i GENERAL QUESTIONS ABOUT YOU

(1) Tell us about yourself. (Aargh!)

What are they really asking?

Your interviewer is assessing what you'd be like to work with. They want to know who you are as a person. You don't have to make it all about the law or academic achievement, but try to focus on the aspects of your personality that demonstrate positive skills for a training contract. Sports and other team activities are great for showing collaborative ability, extra-curricular activities suggest good time management and volunteer work indicates compassion and dedication. What do you want the company to know about you? What aspects of your character define you as a person? Are you an avid reader? A passionate heavy-metal drummer? Do you collect rare maps or restore vintage cars? Say so! All these things make you interesting to be around.

Answers to avoid

Avoid saying that you 'enjoy socialising with friends' or 'don't really have any hobbies'. There *will* be something that makes you stand out. Bring it forward, give it a polish and display it – be memorable!

Sample answer 1:

"I was born in this area so I know the place and the people very well, but I spent two years travelling in South America between college and

university. I did a mix of voluntary work with a healthcare charity and some casual bar and food service work to fund my expedition. I met so many people from all walks of life, and I even started to pick up the language quite well. At university I wrote a regular legal column for the campus newspaper and played cello in the student orchestra. I love reading crime fiction and cooking Italian food."

Note that this answer doesn't mention academic accomplishments or legal work experience at all, but it does paint a picture of a person with some interesting stories and experiences. It also shows that they have local knowledge (very useful in a law firm), can work collaboratively with others (the orchestra) and are self-motivated (working their way around an unfamiliar country). A passion for the law is hinted at with the legal writing for the newspaper, and reading crime fiction. But mainly, it shows the candidate's personality and gives the interviewer a window into their life. Now, work your own story into a similar template – you'll be surprised how great you sound!

Sample answer 2:

"I worked as a chartered surveyor for fifteen years, but I always had an interest in law. I decided in my late thirties to just go for it, so I did a distance-learning degree while working part-time. When I'm not working, I go running and I sometimes help with fundraising events for a local animal rescue charity."

This is a very different answer from the one above, but still demonstrates excellent qualities. Even though this candidate focuses primarily on their career (this is quite normal with candidates who are older or already have some legal work history), they reveal a very positive attitude ('I decided to just go for it!') and the distance learning suggests self-discipline and time management. Fundraising for an animal charity implies a compassionate and caring nature, and the transferable skills from fifteen years as a surveyor would be very valuable in a training contract.

(2) What has been your proudest moment so far?

What are they really asking?

This isn't just about your achievements. It's also about what's important to you in life. It doesn't have to be something big, although if you happen to have conquered Everest then definitely bring it up! Perhaps you overcame your stage fright to play in a piano recital, or you achieved a black belt in kickboxing. Focus on why you're proud of this accomplishment. Did you overcome adversity to achieve a personal goal? Did you confront a fear or self-doubt to do something you didn't think you were capable of? Think about the things that are most memorable to you, and how they came about.

Answers to avoid

Don't say 'getting my degree'! Most people walking into that interview room will give that exact answer. The interviewer already knows you have a degree – they've seen your CV and it's the reason you're there. So be a bit more imaginative – use the opportunity to bring up something they don't already know about you.

If you're a parent, it's tempting to give an answer about how proud you are of your children. Remember that this should be about *you*, and something you've done or accomplished. The answer 'I'm really proud to be a mother/father' doesn't tell the interviewer much about you as a person, even if you *are* the reason they turned out so wonderful!

In some circumstances, however, mentioning children can be appropriate for this question (see sample answers 4 and 5), but don't make your children the entire basis of your answer. You have your own achievements, your own skills and your own personality, and the interview is about you and only you!

Sample answer 1:

"Some of my friends and I set up a fundraiser at uni for the war in Ukraine. We wanted to do something to help, so we got donations of clothing from

students and faculty members and held a fashion show. We raised over £2,000. I was proud because I was able to find a way to help even though I didn't have much money to spare. Also, my friends and I modelled the clothes ourselves, so it was quite a new experience for me to stand up in front of so many people like that. It was something I'll never forget."

Sample answer 2:

"I ran for election for the student body president in my second year, and I was voted in. I was really proud because I put a lot of work into the campaign and it took me right out of my comfort zone. I learned a lot about committees and really got to practise my public speaking skills."

Sample answer 3:

"In my previous job I was promoted to assistant manager. I was proud to be given the position because around thirty other people had applied, and many of them had worked for the company a lot longer than I had. I was given a lot more responsibility, including supervising a team of five. I was later made head of the department."

Sample answer 4:

"I've fostered eleven refugee children in total, and home-schooled them myself. They're all now thriving, happy and independent. I'm proud that I was able to have a valuable impact on these vulnerable youngsters who desperately needed a home and education."

Sample answer 5:

"I'm proud of the fact that, by starting up a small business from home offering copywriting services to marketing companies, I was able to go from a single parent sleeping in a friend's spare room, to a self-sufficient homeowner able to support my child and myself. I'm also proud that I studied part-time for a degree while running my business and looking after a toddler."

(3) Why should we choose you?

What are they really asking?

Exactly what it sounds like! What will the company gain from choosing you? What can you offer? This is the one where you sell yourself, so have those personal unique selling points ready to reel off!

Answers to avoid

This isn't the time to be modest or play down your achievements. Let them know why you would be a great choice.

Sample answer:

"I have a lot of experience dealing with people, from working as a bartender during university and also in my role on the student council. My communication and customer service skills are strong, so you could put me in front of clients straight away and I'll give a good impression. I'm a fast learner so I would very quickly become a productive member of the team. I'm punctual, and I get along well with people. Working in a bar has also given me excellent multi-tasking skills and I'm used to getting things done under pressure."

(4) What are your strengths?

What are they really asking?

This is about the unique skill set you'll bring to the role. It's also an assessment of your self-awareness. It's an easy one to have ready if you prepare in advance, so reflect on where your strengths are and plan your answer beforehand, because this question is guaranteed to come up in one form or another!

Answers to avoid

Never say that you don't know what your strengths are. Everyone has strong points, and you must be able to identify what you're good at. Some excellent answers from training contract candidates include compassion, energy, empathy, flexibility and local knowledge!

Sample answer 1:

"I think my biggest strength is resilience. I come from a relatively humble background and nobody in my family had been to university. I had to study for my degree whilst also working full time, and there were more than a few setbacks along the way. It was so important to me, though, that I had to persevere even when I felt like I couldn't do it. It was worth the effort and it may not have meant so much if I'd had an easier path, so I'm really glad I stuck with it. It's also made me a lot more aware of what others may be going through at any time, and I always try to treat people kindly and help others whenever I can."

Sample answer 2:

"I'm good at solving problems. I think it's because of my background in I.T., but I've always found that I can solve quite tricky problems really quickly. I've got a very analytical mind, so I'm also good at spotting alternative ways of solving the same issue. When I did my law degree, I found that I always got very high marks in problem questions, so I think it's a character trait that will carry across really well to the legal profession."

(5) What are your weaknesses?

What are they really asking?

This question is less about listing the things you're not very good at, and more about your attitude to self-improvement.

Answers to avoid

There are some very cliché answers to this question that will just make your interviewer cringe. Don't say 'I'm a perfectionist and I never stop working!' It just doesn't sound genuine. A better way to turn a negative question into a positive answer is to focus instead on areas you've improved on recently.

Sample answer 1:

"I realised when I started working in financial administration that my I.T. skills could be stronger, so I did a short course through the local adult learning centre. It focused on MS Office and especially Excel, which is the programme I was least comfortable with. Now I know a lot more about its functions and I use it every day in my current job. It's actually really sped up my workflow."

Sample answer 2:

"I always found it difficult to meet deadlines for assignments, and it became a bit of a running joke at college. When I did my master's degree, I had to become much more disciplined at managing my time, and I started to really focus on getting the work done early. It's so much less stressful now that I've got into the habit of planning and scheduling. I use a virtual whiteboard to organise my time and it really helps me keep control of all my commitments."

Sample answer 3:

"One of the things I'm working on is being more willing to delegate. I've always been quite fiercely independent and don't really like asking for help. Working on group projects on the LPC has recently helped

me improve in this regard, though, and working in teams has certainly helped me to accept that I don't always have to do everything myself, and everyone has different things to contribute."

Sample answer 4:

"Sometimes I try to do things too quickly, and I've had to learn to slow down so that I don't make mistakes. I like to be efficient and get a lot done in a day, and working in retail you do tend to develop a tendency towards speediness. Studying law has really underlined for me how important it is to take things a little more cautiously and check everything over, because rushing leads to mistakes, and mistakes in law can have catastrophic consequences. Especially in exam situations, I've learned to read the questions much more slowly, and more than once, before starting my answers."

 ☆NOTES☆

(6) What will you bring to the company?

What are they really asking?

A variation on 'Why should we choose you?' Don't be surprised if this question comes up more than once in slightly different wording. **If you have a good network of contacts, make sure you say so. Law firms like to know if you'll bring new business to the company.**

Answers to avoid

Avoid stating the qualities that every candidate will bring, such as legal knowledge! Use examples that make you stand out.

Sample answer:

"I'll bring a lot of enthusiasm and energy, as well as my skills in solving client problems, which I gained during my time as a volunteer for Citizens Advice. I have extensive local knowledge, as I've lived in the area for most of my life, and would bring this knowledge into my conveyancing seat. I also have a reasonable circle of entrepreneurial friends and I would hope to bring many of them on board as business clients in the future."

(7) What would your colleagues or peers say about you?

What are they really asking?

This is another way of gaining insight into your character, and is a good opportunity to throw in some positive personality traits.

Answers to avoid

Try to avoid bragging. 'My friends would say I'm really clever and kind and I'm very hard-working' sounds a bit too false. Also avoid anything that may not be attractive to a legal recruiter. 'They'd say I'm a party animal and a bit of a wild child. I'm always the centre of attention' is not the impression to go for in an interview!

Sample answer:

"They'd probably say that I'm easy to get along with. I'm usually the one my friends call on in a crisis because I'll always try to help and I don't get overwhelmed easily. I'm probably the sensible one of the group, but I do like to have fun as well."

 ☆NOTES☆

★ TOP TIPS ★

DRESS PROFESSIONALLY, BUT COMFORTABLY

It's better to err on the side of too formal than too casual. A dark-coloured suit and smart shoes is a safe bet. Although many firms now embrace a more relaxed culture, the legal profession as a whole is not renowned for being forward-thinking and modern. Even if you know the firm you're interviewing for has a casual dress code, you should still dress formally for the interview. Plain trousers or skirt and a smart top, with smart, clean shoes, at the very least. Do avoid wearing shoes that pinch or a shirt that's too small, as you'll be distracted by your own discomfort, and you need to be comfortable enough to concentrate on the conversation. For example, if you're not used to wearing high heels, an interview isn't the best time to test your balance with six-inch stilettos! Flat shoes are absolutely fine (and any company that insists on ladies wearing high heels for work is probably not a company you want to work for, anyway – you're not auditioning for Suits!). Oh, and don't overdo the perfume/aftershave!

★ NOTES ★

(8) Tell me about your work history.

What are they really asking?

Your interviewer already has your CV, so they're not looking for a recap of your employment to date. They want to hear your take on your experiences so far, what has been important to you in your career and what transferable skills you've gained. What influences you? Do you make sensible career choices? Did someone tell you that you'd make a good lawyer? What are your goals?

Answers to avoid

Don't just reel off a list of the places you've worked and your job titles, and don't say that you just drifted or fell into any of your previous roles. Give some insight into skills you've developed, jobs you've enjoyed and what you've learned.

Sample answer 1:

"I started off working part-time in retail while I was at college. It was very fast-paced and gave me a good set of skills to get a foot on the job ladder, so after that I progressed into administrative work and have been doing that for the last five years. During that time I've completed several management and leadership courses and a diploma in business finance. I went part-time to retrain in the law when I realised that I really enjoyed detail-oriented and client-focused work. My office manager encouraged me to go and do a law degree because they thought I had the right mindset, and I'm very glad they did!"

Sample answer 2:

"I only finished university this summer, so my work experience has comprised mainly part-time bar work, and two vacation schemes. One was at a corporate City firm, another was a volunteer role at the uni's legal advice clinic, so quite different experiences. I loved the variety of work at the City firm and the culture really appealed to me – I love to be busy all the time so the frantic pace quite suited me. At the same time, though, it

was incredibly rewarding to be able to help people at the law clinic who didn't otherwise have access to legal assistance. I enjoyed both placements immensely, and although they were very different environments, they both made me realise that I'd love to specialise in litigation eventually."

 **NOTES**

(9) What are your hobbies?

What are they really asking?

Here the interviewer is looking for a number of things: your level of enthusiasm for your interests outside of work; whether you manage your time well enough to commit to other activities; have you developed transferable skills through your extracurricular activities, such as teamwork, or a second or third language? It's also a glimpse into your personality.

Answers to avoid

Avoid saying you don't have any hobbies! Also, try to avoid using hobby-specific jargon that the person interviewing you may not understand.

Sample answer:

"I'm a member of an amateur dramatics society. We meet twice a month and put on a show every year. It's great fun and it's really improved my confidence to get up on stage and perform in front of people. It helps me unwind, too – the people are all different ages and we always have a great laugh together."

 NOTES

(10) How do you like to relax?

What are they really asking?

This is a variation on the hobbies question, but also delves into your awareness of self-care and methods for coping with stress.

Answers to avoid

If your way of relaxing is to lie in bed and play games on your phone, that's absolutely fine, but perhaps not the best answer in a job interview. One candidate answered this question with 'I just have a few beers'. They didn't get the job.

Sample answer 1:

"If I feel the need to unwind or recharge my batteries, I often go for a long hike in the hills somewhere and just enjoy being out in nature and the fresh air. It helps to clear my mind and gives me chance to think if I need to, without distractions."

Sample answer 2:

"I find gardening very relaxing and therapeutic. I try to get out in the garden most weekends and that's how I unwind. It's great for relieving stress. If the weather's bad I go for a swim instead, or just out for coffee with friends."

☆NOTES☆

(11) How are your numeracy skills?

Answers to avoid

Don't say that they're bad! You'll need reasonable numeracy skills for any legal job, so find a positive. If you run a household to a budget, you have numeracy skills. If you've worked in retail or any job handling money, you have numeracy skills. You don't need to have a degree in advanced mathematics – life experience is rife with examples of everyday numeracy.

Sample answer 1:

"I'm confident dealing with money and working out my own budget. I know I'll need to produce completion statements and invoices in this role, and work out stamp duty, and I know that my maths skills are definitely up to this."

Sample answer 2:

"My numeracy skills are fairly strong. In my previous job I was responsible for cashing up at the end of the shift so I had to have a reasonable head for figures. I always check everything with a calculator to be on the safe side, but my mental arithmetic is quite sound."

Sample answer 3:

"I enjoy a game of darts with friends on a Sunday evening. It's a game where you're constantly doing maths and I usually get the task of keeping score because I'm quick with mental arithmetic."

(12) How well do you get along with your colleagues?

What are they really asking?

They want to know if you'll be a good person to work with and whether you'll be a good fit for the team.

Answers to avoid

If there's someone at work you don't get along with, or if you simply don't like any of your colleagues, this isn't the time to air those particular views. If you come across as frosty, difficult or antisocial, it's unlikely you'll be asked back.

Sample answer:

"I get on well with my workmates. We're all from quite different backgrounds, although we can usually find some common interests. I'm quite easy-going and I like working with others, so I usually get along with people generally and don't find myself in confrontations."

(13) Would you say that you have good attention to detail?

Sample answer 1:

"Yes. I'm very detail-oriented so I tend to spot things. In my current job I'm responsible for proofreading all our marketing material. I've always had an eye for detail."

Sample answer 2:

"Yes. I like to paint watercolours, so I've always been observant for little details – no matter how small."

Sample answer 3:

"Yes. I grew up reading Sherlock Holmes with my dad. He encouraged me, very early on, to be observant because you never know when it might be important."

 **NOTES**

(14) How do you motivate others?

What are they really asking?

This is a variation on leadership qualities. Will you be future partner material? Will you inspire your colleagues? Will you be a positive force within the team?

Sample answer:

"I believe in leading by example, so I would never expect anyone to do something I wouldn't be willing to do myself. I previously managed a cleaning company, and if we were short-staffed I'd be there with my toilet brush and mop, mucking in. I think the best way to motivate is to encourage and praise. People like to know their efforts have been noted and appreciated, and they also like to be consulted where appropriate. If someone makes a mistake or is doing something wrong, I'd let them know how to improve and give them the tools to do so, such as extra training or assistance. I wouldn't just tell them they're getting it wrong and make them feel stupid. I always try to use positive language and encouragement."

(15) How do you cope under pressure?

Answers to avoid

Avoid saying that you get stressed easily, or that you cry or get angry. If you do struggle under pressure, think about coping strategies that you've found to work, and use those as examples.

Sample answer:

"My current job can be quite stressful at times, but I try to stay calm and tackle things logically and rationally. If the pressure is just sheer volume of work, I'll look at what needs to be done and prioritise my tasks in order of urgency. If it's possible to delegate, I'll ask for help so that clients aren't left waiting. I think sometimes it's easy to mistake being busy for being stressed, so keeping things in perspective and planning ahead as much as possible is very important in a busy environment. If I start to feel really overwhelmed, I sometimes use breathing exercises to help me refocus and maintain control, and that really helps ease the pressure."

(16) Can you describe yourself in five words?

What are they really asking?

This is simply a variation on the 'Tell me about yourself' theme, but with an added test of thinking on your feet. You can (and should) prepare descriptions of yourself in advance, because you'll definitely be asked this in some form. If you've already identified the characteristics you want to shine a light on, you can rattle off answers to these questions without missing a beat!

Answers to avoid

There are no right or wrong answers to this question as such. It's more about how you handle the question. Don't over-think it. How *would* you describe yourself? How would your friends, family, tutors or colleagues describe you?

Sample answer 1:

"Studious, caring, reader, ambitious, animal-lover."

Sample answer 2:

"Confident, outgoing, positive, dedicated, resilient."

Sample answer 3:

"Determined, optimistic, loyal, attentive, honest."

☆NOTES☆———————

(17) What would the person who knows you best say is your worst quality?

What are they really asking?

A variation on 'What are your weaknesses?' This is a good one to prepare ahead of the interview as it will almost always come up.

Answers to avoid

The reality may be that your closest friend might say you're over-sensitive, or your parents would say you have a tendency towards laziness. There is a way of making faults sound less negative, and again it's about being aware of your own improvements, but make sure you have an answer ready. Saying that you don't have any negative qualities suggests that you are, at best, arrogant, and at worst, untruthful!

Sample answer 1:

"My dad used to say I didn't push myself enough. At school I tended not to try out for sports teams because I didn't think I was good enough, but I realise now I wasn't actually that bad. Going to uni really helped raise my confidence levels and belief in my abilities. I definitely don't hold myself back now. That's why I applied for this position at a top Legal 500 firm. I'm confident I have the potential to be a successful corporate lawyer and I have the drive and the determination to achieve that goal."

Sample answer 2:

"Some of my friends have described me as quiet, but I'm definitely not a shy person. I'm just more of a listener. I'm not afraid to speak up when I have something to say, and I can chat about pretty much anything with anyone. I'm just not really one for nattering."

Sample answer 3:

"You may have heard the phrase 'a painting is never finished, merely abandoned'? I used to have a problem with letting go – always tweaking. A creative writing course I attended a few years ago really helped me to

recognise the point when a project is viable and stopped me from going down that road of diminishing returns. It was a valuable lesson and I think it translates well into the business and professional worlds, where time is money."

(18) Would you say you have good communication skills? Can you give an example?

Sample answer 1:

"Yes, I'd say that communication is one of my strong points. I always did well in mooting and advocacy workshops at university, and I seem to have a good flair for persuasion. In my final year I entered a debating competition and I had to argue against something I was personally strongly in favour of, and I won."

Sample answer 2:

"My communication skills are very good. I've volunteered at a law clinic for almost two years, so I've had the opportunity to really build on these skills as I gave advice on the phone, in person and in writing or by email. I learned to use language to suit the intended audience and not overwhelm people with legal jargon or too much case law or statute, which was very different from the assignments for my law degree. I also had to check everything carefully for accuracy, and make sure there were no spelling or grammar errors in the written advice. It's really honed my oral and written communication skills and it was a very rewarding experience at the same time."

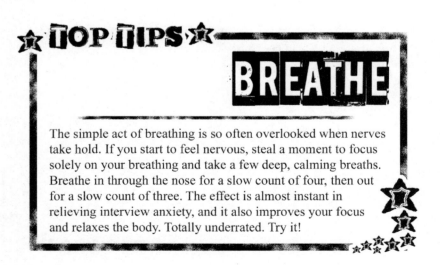

☆ TOP TIPS ☆

BREATHE

The simple act of breathing is so often overlooked when nerves take hold. If you start to feel nervous, steal a moment to focus solely on your breathing and take a few deep, calming breaths. Breathe in through the nose for a slow count of four, then out for a slow count of three. The effect is almost instant in relieving interview anxiety, and it also improves your focus and relaxes the body. Totally underrated. Try it!

NOTES

(19) Are you an extrovert or an introvert?

Sample answer 1:

"I'm quite an outgoing person. I enjoy meeting new people and I like to hear their stories and experiences. I'm quite chatty, so probably more of an extrovert, which has come in useful in my previous job where I staffed the company's stand at trade shows. It was good to be able to just build a rapport with people and get a conversation going, rather than just handing out leaflets. It made the whole experience more rewarding."

Sample answer 2:

"I'm not sure I'd describe myself as an introvert exactly. I do enjoy other people's company – I'm just more of a listener than a talker. That said, my public speaking skills are good and I have no qualms about speaking up and contributing to group projects."

Sample answer 3:

"Neither one nor the other. I'm not a wallflower, but I wouldn't call myself the life and soul of the party, either. I'm happy in my own company or in a group, and I generally get along well with people. I find I can chat about anything and everything, but am equally happy sitting in the garden with a good book."

★NOTES★

(20) What is the one thing that sets you apart from other candidates?

What are they really asking?

Here's your chance to tell the interviewer, straight out, why they should pick you and not the next person. Grab the opportunity with both hands. Set out your strongest skills, your character traits and why you'd be not only a fantastic trainee solicitor but a great person to have around the office!

Answers to avoid

Try to avoid run-of-the-mill answers such as 'I'm a hard worker'. Focus on two or three things that make you the best person for the role.

Sample answer 1:

"I already have several years of work experience. Even though this was in the publishing industry, you won't need to wait for me to learn the basics – I can communicate effectively, use client management software and I'm used to using my own initiative and researching information if I don't know something. I think that gives me a good head-start over candidates coming straight from academia. I have an excellent work ethic and I'm very good at motivating others. I think I'd be a positive and helpful presence on the team."

Sample answer 2:

"The thing that sets me apart is, I think, my attitude. I'm extremely resilient and tenacious, and I believe I have the drive and determination to be a valuable member of the firm from the outset. Throughout my degree I battled illness, bereavement and a family break-up, but I still showed up, got the work done and came out with an upper second. I don't let setbacks stop me or hold me back. I'll bring that resolve and determination to the traineeship and always give my best."

Sample answer 3:

"All my skills and qualifications relate very well to the job description for the training contract. On top of that, I have a particular skill for networking and over the last ten years of running my own business I've built up a strong base of contacts. I'd aim to bring those contacts on board as new business clients. I'd also continue to attend chamber of commerce meetings and promote the firm at any appropriate opportunity. I believe my people skills, most of all, set me apart from other candidates."

Sample answer 4:

"I've never believed in 'that'll do'. I'm always willing to go the extra mile, a diligence that's been noted throughout my education, all the way back to school. I believe that attention to detail makes me an ideal candidate for this training contract and for a legal career with this firm in the long term."

ii CAREER QUESTIONS

(21) Where do you see yourself in five (or ten) years' time?

What are they really asking?

Employing a trainee solicitor is an investment, and the recruiter will want to make sure that their investment in you is going to be worthwhile, and that you won't move on as soon as you qualify (or sooner). As part of your training contract, you'll need to complete the Professional Skills Course (PSC) at your employer's expense, and the company will need to invest time and resources in training you to the SRA's standards. In a nutshell, they want to know if you plan to stick around!

Sample answer:

"I really enjoyed the civil litigation module on the LPC, so that may be an area I'd like to qualify into after completing my training contract seats, but I'm keeping my options open. I know that litigation is a big part of the firm's business, and from what I've seen so far I'd like to think that in five/ten years' time I'll be here, having taken a few steps up the career ladder by then and perhaps eventually leading a department."

(22) Why are you leaving your current job?

What are they really asking?

Most people have a genuine reason for leaving their job, and in most cases for training contract applicants the answer will simply be that you've completed your professional qualifications and now you're looking to start your legal career. For career changers, the recruiter will want to know whether you find it difficult to get along with colleagues or managers, or if you tend to move from job to job without staying long.

Answers to avoid

Avoid saying that you don't like your boss or the company you work for. It may well be the case, but it could make you come across as difficult or unfriendly. It's also best not to say that you're bored with your work.

Sample answer 1:

"I've really enjoyed my time in hotel management, and the feedback I've had from the directors has always been very positive. I made the commitment to retrain as a solicitor because I felt that it fit better with my particular skills and goals, and now that I've completed the GDL and LPC I'm ready to take the next step and start my training contract. I'm sure the skills I've learned over the last few years will transfer very well to a career in law."

Sample answer 2:

"I've been lucky to have such a good employer, but they're a medium-sized, family-run business, so there's little or no opportunity for further growth within the company. I have, and will retain, a good relationship with them, but believe I can achieve more of my potential and goals as part of this firm, going forward. All the skills I gained in my previous employment are transferable and I've worked so hard to achieve the qualifications I now have, that I feel it's time to make the move. I'm really excited about getting my teeth into a career with wider opportunities."

(23) Do you prefer working alone or in a group?

Sample answer 1:

"I'm very self-motivated so I'm quite happy to just get on with a task on my own, and I'm good at using my own initiative rather than needing my hand held constantly, but I also really enjoyed working in groups on the GDL for collaborative exercises. I like bouncing ideas off others and coming up with things I may not have thought of on my own."

Sample answer 2:

"Both are rewarding. I certainly get a feeling of satisfaction when I've solved a problem or achieved a goal on my own, but working with others can often be enjoyable, even fun. It's a good way to learn, too. I'd have to say I'm comfortable with either."

☆**NOTES**☆

(24) What are your expectations from this role?

Sample answer 1:

"It goes without saying that I want to qualify as a solicitor, but I'd also like the opportunity to take on more responsibility further down the line, and specialise in mergers and acquisitions. I have some experience as a paralegal in a large corporate firm and I'd love to build on that. I know that this company has a very hands-on approach to training and so I anticipate that you'll have high expectations of me from the start, but that the quality of legal training will be extremely high too. Ultimately, I'd like to join the mergers team and build a good network of my own clients once qualified."

Sample answer 2:

"After qualifying, I'd like to move further into commercial property law – it's one of the reasons I applied to this firm. My intention is to become a specialist in that area and grow within this company. Throughout my education, I've captained sports teams and worked towards leadership roles within various student groups and movements. I hope to build on that experience to eventually take on a leadership role within this company in the future."

(25) Have you applied/interviewed at any other firms? Which ones?

What are they really asking?

The reasons for asking this question are twofold. It's to see whether you've genuinely done your research and are keen to work at that particular firm, or whether you've simply sent applications to every law firm within a 10-mile radius. It also gives the interviewer a heads-up if a particularly good candidate is likely to be snapped up by a rival. Even if you're a 'blanket-bomber' applicant (which we don't recommend, by the way), the etiquette within the legal profession is to imply that the company you're interviewing for is your first choice and your personal Holy Grail.

Answers to avoid

It's fine to say that you've applied elsewhere, but don' t make it sound as though they're just one in a pile of hundreds.

Sample answer:

"I spent a long time researching companies that had a strong focus on family law, and then narrowed down my choices by attending law fairs and talking to current staff and trainees. I refined it to three companies that I felt had a good ethos and whose staff seemed motivated and enthusiastic, and applied to those three. This firm is my first choice because it's exactly the type of work I want to specialise in, the team are really friendly and you have by far the best client reviews in the area."

51

(26) What motivates you in your work?

Sample answer 1:

"I decided to study law because I enjoy working with people, and I like solving complex problems. Being able to help people is what motivates me because I find it really rewarding. I volunteered at a legal advice clinic last summer and it confirmed for me that I really want to help resolve legal issues that are affecting people's everyday life, and in some cases their mental health. Seeing the relief when you tell someone you can help them with their problem is fantastic."

Sample answer 2:

"I was always quite competitive academically and I am definitely motivated by success. I like to do as well as I possibly can and to have my achievements recognised. I always strive to be the best, and that's what motivates me in my work, too."

Sample answer 3:

"I really enjoy solving legal challenges. The sense of triumph when I have an answer, or an unbeatable argument, within a litigation case, is what I live for!"

✯NOTES✯

★ TOP TIPS ★

TURN NEGATIVES INTO POSITIVES

Instead of saying "I'm not going anywhere with my current job and I just don't enjoy it any more", turn it around and talk about what you DO want from your job. "I've really enjoyed my time at Folk Law and I've learned some valuable skills. Now I'm looking to move into a more senior role where I can develop my leadership abilities and I'm ready for something new and exciting."

★ NOTES ★

53

(27) Why did you choose that university?

What are they really asking?

This isn't a judgment on the university you went to! It's to assess how you make decisions, how you reflect on those decisions and what's important to you.

Sample answer:

"I started by reading prospectuses, particularly from the top ten universities on the Times rankings for Law. I narrowed it down to the ones that had work placement programmes, because I wanted to make sure I gained some practical experience during the course, and I went to open days at those five. I was really pleased to be offered a conditional place at my first choice because the Law programme was superb. All the tutors were established solicitors or barristers, and the environment was very relaxed and upbeat compared to some of the other universities I visited. It was definitely the right fit for me and I loved my time there."

 ☆NOTES☆

(28) What areas of law are you interested in?

What are they really asking?

From a business perspective, an interviewer at a shipping law firm isn't going to recruit a candidate who says they're most interested in family law! Make sure your specialist areas tie in with the firm's main disciplines.

Sample answer:

"I found the Private Client module of the LPC really interesting. I'd like to specialise in estate planning and trusts eventually. I know the firm's two main areas of expertise are conveyancing and private client, and as I also did well in the property law exams, I'd be keen to spend time in both areas."

 NOTES

(29) Are there any areas of law that don't interest you?

What are they really asking?

This isn't a trick question. Your interviewer will be determining whether you have the enthusiasm for that particular company's specialisms.

Answers to avoid

Again, make sure you don't say that you hate business law if you're applying to a corporate firm – obviously!

Sample answer:

"My least favourite module was criminal litigation. I got good marks in the exams and some of it was very thought-provoking, but it's just not an area I'm interested in pursuing as a career. That's one of the reasons I've applied here, as this firm doesn't undertake any criminal work."

 **NOTES**

(30) What sort of experience do you have in advocacy?

Sample answer 1:

"I was a member of the mooting society for two years, and that's really helped develop my skills of persuasion and speaking in public. I also volunteered at a law clinic last summer, and I had to negotiate with creditors on behalf of some of our debt clients."

Sample answer 2:

"In one of my previous roles I worked for a mental health charity. Part of the job was dealing with benefits applications and appeals on behalf of service users. Sometimes this was in person, but usually by phone or video call. I had to prepare case notes, go through evidence documents and present arguments to the panel or tribunal."

 **NOTES**

(31) What attracted you to this firm's training contract programme? How do you think we are different from our competitors?

What are they really asking?

They want to see if you've genuinely paid attention to the company and done your homework. This is an easy one to have ready, so make sure you prepare your answers ahead of time.

Answers to avoid

One candidate once answered this question by saying that it was the closest law firm to where they lived, so they wouldn't have far to travel. While this may be a factor in your decision, it's not what the interviewer wants to hear!

Sample answer:

"I've read the recruitment literature and I noted that over 90% of your trainees stay on after their training contract, so that tells me a lot about working here. Speaking to two of your newly qualified solicitors at a law fair recently gave me a very positive insight into the culture at the company, and I feel it would be an excellent fit. I'm looking for somewhere I can progress in my career, and I'm aware that you regularly promote high-achieving associates. I think the biggest difference between this firm and your closest competitors is that your competitors have a higher staff turnover, and there doesn't seem to be as much opportunity for progression."

(32) Do you have any client-facing experience?

Sample answer 1:

"Yes, I've worked on reception at a housing association. A big part of that job was dealing with customers, contractors and service providers. I was usually the first point of contact, so it was important to create a good first impression on everyone who walked through the door, and to communicate clearly and respectfully. I'd have no concerns about dealing with clients and taking a lead in client interviews – it doesn't faze me at all."

Sample answer 2:

"My work experience during university wasn't client-facing, although I did of course interact with my colleagues and supervisors. I don't think this will be a disadvantage, though. The LPC programme is very practical in nature and there are lots of role-playing scenarios for the advocacy and client interviewing assessments, so I've had some practice. I'm naturally a very approachable and friendly person and I find talking to people quite easy. My manner is professional and polite, and I think I'd take to this aspect of the job role very quickly."

(33) What experience do you have in dealing with large amounts of money?

What are they really asking?

Law firms are under strict regulation when it comes to money laundering awareness, as you'll know from your legal studies. The interviewer wants to see that you appreciate the serious role this plays in legal transactions.

Sample answer:

"I was treasurer of the student association for a year, and I was responsible for keeping meticulous records and checking the accounts regularly. I'm very careful when it comes to dealing with finances and as a trainee, I would be vigilant about checking sources of client funds and carrying out proper ID checks."

★ **TOP TIPS** ★

BODY LANGUAGE

Be aware of your posture and try not to slouch. Leaning forward slightly is a sign of engagement and enthusiasm. Avoid crossing your arms as this is defensive body language and creates a subconscious 'barrier' between you and the interviewer. Be aware of your facial expressions. Demonstrate active listening when the interviewer is explaining something to you: nodding, acknowledging, smiling and verbal reinforcements such as 'I see', 'right', or summarising and clarifying what has been said, are all indicators of great listening skills and will be noted.

NOTES

(34) How would you feel about being supervised or told what to do by someone younger than you?

Sample answer 1:

"As I've made the decision to change careers in my thirties, it's probably inevitable that some of the people who are further ahead in the legal profession are also going to be younger than me. This is absolutely fine and not a concern to me at all. I was one of the oldest students on the LPC but I got along well with the other students and made some wonderful friends. I really don't think age matters. I'm keen to learn, and I appreciate that that doesn't necessarily mean the person teaching me will be older than I am."

Sample answer 2:

"I'm a career changer, so it will come as no surprise if some of the solicitors I work with are younger than myself. They will be more experienced in the law, and I'm here to learn, to be the best solicitor I can be."

(35) How come you didn't study law?

What are they really asking?

Don't be put off by questions that seem to be worded in a slightly negative way. Interviewers will sometimes throw this type of question in to see how you react and how you handle it.

Answers to avoid

Don't fall into the trap of becoming defensive or getting flustered. You're not justifying your decisions, just explaining them.

Sample answer:

"I chose A-levels in subjects I was good at, which set me on a languages path. It's a useful skill to have but limited in job options. I didn't want to go into politics, and translation work is surprisingly low-paid with very little opportunity for progression. It wasn't until a friend suggested I'd have made a good lawyer that I even really thought about it as a career path. I decided to take an entry-level law module and found I absolutely loved it, so I did the GDL conversion course. I really feel like I found my calling, and although in some ways I wish I'd done it sooner, I do feel that my experience and skills as a freelance interpreter will carry across very well to the modern, global legal profession."

 NOTES

(36) Why didn't you go to university straight after school or college?

Sample answer 1:

"At the time, university wasn't right for me as I wasn't sure at that point what I really wanted to do. It would also have been a huge struggle for my family to afford it, so I went to work to contribute to the family home. I'm glad I went into retail management and gained that experience before deciding on the path to law. It was difficult in many ways going back into education after 15 years, but I got so much more out of it than I would have done if I'd jumped straight in at 18 when I wasn't ready. At this stage in my development, I had the focus and stability to work hard and achieve my goals, so I'm glad I did it a bit later in life. It was absolutely worth the wait."

Sample answer 2:

"A university education wasn't necessary for my original employment plans. Later, and after several years' experience, I questioned my original choice and found my interests turning towards the law. After reading around the subject, I signed up to a distance learning degree, and very quickly, it felt like coming home. Now, I'm really enthusiastic about my future in the law."

★ NOTES ★

☆ TOP TIPS ☆

I DON'T KNOW

'I don't know' is a perfectly acceptable answer. Interviewers can detect a bluff at a hundred paces, so don't try to brazen it out! Instead, be as positive as you can, or give a hypothetical answer:

"That's a situation I haven't yet had to deal with, but I think in those circumstances I would..."

"I'm not familiar with that particular legislation, but I'm keen to learn and I do pick things up very quickly."

"I haven't come across that concept before - please could you clarify?"

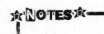

(37) You've done well in your degree and the LPC/SQE but your grades at school are lower than we usually see. Is there a reason for that?

What are they really asking?

They're asking whether there are genuine reasons for the results you obtained. They will also be paying attention to how you handle failure or setbacks.

Answers to avoid

Avoid giving answers that sound defensive or dismissive. If there are genuine reasons, be honest, and then focus on your later successes.

Sample answer 1:

"It was disappointing because I worked hard and thought I'd revised well enough. I'm not sure exactly why I didn't do as well as I was capable of doing – although I think perhaps I tried to memorise too much detail and neglected the broader picture in some subjects. At college I became a lot better at note-taking and consolidating my understanding, so my grades improved significantly and I was able to achieve a First in my law degree. It was a learning curve for me."

Sample answer 2:

"I had a difficult time at school and was bullied quite badly, which affected my studies. After leaving school I went into the job market, made a new circle of friends and found myself, so to speak. Although I initially thought my chance for higher education had passed me by, I found that I really enjoyed helping people. I came across a recruitment advert for law school, and it chimed instantly with me. I continued my work, but registered for distance learning and found that I loved it. I now have no doubt that my future will be in the law, and in helping people."

**NOTES**

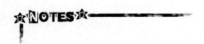 **NOTES**

iii LAW QUESTIONS

(38) Why did you choose to study law?

Sample answer 1:

"I always wanted to be a lawyer. When I was at school I did work experience in a law firm and it was exactly what I'd imagined. I loved it. I went to college and studied law and then applied for the law programme at Exeter. Now I'm looking to start my training contract with a company that has a broad range of legal services so that I can work out exactly which area of law I'd like to specialise in when I qualify."

Sample answer 2:

"I studied history at university because I enjoyed the subject, but didn't really have a clear career path in mind. While I was at uni, I got involved with the debating society and met several members of the law faculty. The idea of working in the legal profession really started to appeal to me. I liked the problem-solving aspects, and the history of the development of the legal system has always fascinated me. I realised I wanted to pursue law as a career and so I did the conversion course."

(39) If you could pass one new law, what would it be?

What are they really asking?

Questions like this are designed to assess how well you can think on your feet. Try to come up with an intelligent and sensible answer that you can justify if the interviewer has follow-up questions.

Answers to avoid

Most lawyers have strong opinions – it goes with the territory – but in an interview situation it's best to avoid any topics that might be considered controversial. One unfortunate candidate answered this question by saying that they would ban all domestic pets. The recruiter was an avid animal lover.

Sample answer 1:

"I think one of the biggest problems currently is homelessness and a lack of available accommodation. I would legislate so that empty, habitable buildings couldn't remain unoccupied for more than, say, six months without good reason, and I'd make it compulsory that they be used for accommodation for those most in need. If the owners then secured a legitimate use for the building they could apply to repossess it, on the proviso that the person living there is found somewhere else to go beforehand."

Sample answer 2:

"When I was studying tort law I always thought that, in reality, the laws on misrepresentation are difficult to enforce. There's been a huge increase in frauds and scams recently, especially targeting the elderly, and they're becoming ever more sophisticated. I'd make deliberately lying to deceive someone a criminal offence, and make it simpler for victims of scammers to obtain recompense and justice."

(40) What do you know about this firm?

What are they really asking?

Are you genuinely interested in this firm, or is this one of many cut-and-paste applications? Try to throw in a detail that can't be gleaned from a quick skim through the website, if possible.

Sample answer:

"I know that the company has been around for over 70 years and has a good local reputation. You have eleven full-time staff and offer conveyancing, wills and probate and private client work, but also sometimes take on low-value debt recovery. When I spoke to your current trainee at a law fair, they told me that the senior partner is an avid guitarist and loves Iron Maiden!"

 **NOTES**

(41) For what reasons might clients choose to hold a property as tenants in common instead of joint tenants?

What are they really asking?

You're more likely to come across 'test' questions like this at larger firms. The interviewer wants to recruit the best and the brightest, as well as the right personality types.

Answers to avoid

Don't be flustered – they're not trick questions, and the interviewer isn't trying to trip you up. They will usually be a fairly easy legal question, so take your time and don't over-think it.

Sample answer:

"The main reasons would be so that they can leave their share to whomever they choose in their will, rather than ownership passing by survivorship. There may be strategic inheritance tax reasons for not wanting their share to go to each other. Or, it could be that a property is owned by a small group of students, for example, rather than a couple, and it wouldn't be appropriate in that case to hold as joint tenants. A tenancy in common is also a more practical way of holding property where the owners have contributed unequal shares, or want to specify the proportions of their respective ownership."

(42) What is the most valuable thing you learned while studying law?

Your answer need not necessarily be *about* the law. Look back and contemplate: what stood out for you as the most important thing you learned? Your answer will be personal to you.

Sample answer:

"The biggest thing for me was probably learning to manage my workload. My organisation and time management skills really improved during my three years at university. I found it quite difficult at first to keep on top of so many assignment deadlines, as the workload was much heavier than at college, but I've learned how to plan effectively and use my time well."

(43) Have you always wanted to be a lawyer?

Sample answer 1:

"Yes, *always. I've been fascinated by criminal law ever since I was young, and I thought I'd become a barrister. When I started studying law in college, I realised I was more suited to the role of a solicitor and decided to undertake the LPC instead of the Bar Training Course.*"

Sample answer 2:

"*I always knew I wanted to do something that would make good use of my academic abilities. Originally, I thought I'd go into teaching. I'm good at explaining things clearly and I'm a very patient person, but I became interested in law at college and decided this was a much better career path for me. I don't have any regrets about not becoming a teacher.*"

☆NOTES☆

Academic performance and experience are obviously important, but the interviewer is also assessing your potential as a 'fit' for the company. If they feel their people might be uncomfortable with you around, that can be a distinct disadvantage for you when trying to land a training contract. Even if you're feeling nervous on the day, simply making the effort to smile and make eye contact gives a much warmer impression than the candidate who doesn't. Remember, they're choosing someone they're going to be spending at least eight hours a day with, so smile! Easy points!

(44) Why have you chosen this area of law?

Sample answer 1:

"I want to go into family law to make a difference. Having been through the process of a family law case, I appreciate what an impact it makes to have a strong and knowledgeable advocate on side. It's important to me to be able to help people and to make that difference. If I didn't go into family law, I would also be interested in mental health law for the same reasons."

Sample answer 2:

"I thrive in a busy, fast-paced environment. I want a job where no two days are the same – that's why I've chosen corporate law. I'm a very energetic person and I like to be fully immersed in a task. Deadlines motivate me, and I have a good understanding of the business world. I've chosen corporate law simply because it suits my personality. I know it's not for everyone, but I flourish in an active and demanding role."

(45) I see you've worked in HR for the last five years. Why the change to law now?

What are they really asking?

They want to be sure you've considered your decision carefully and are not someone who rushes from job to job, or even career to career. Your answer will need to show that you gave proper thought to your decision and did your research before jumping into something new.

Answers to avoid

Avoid saying that you're bored in your work or that you just fancied a change.

Sample answer:

"I've thoroughly enjoyed my years in HR and I've met some incredible people. The training courses I attended were first-class and gave me a solid grounding in people skills and team leadership, which I'm sure I'll use effectively as a trainee solicitor. Over the years, I became more and more interested in the employment law side of the job, and I found myself doing more professional development in this area, voluntarily. One of my managers suggested that I look into qualifying as an employment solicitor. The company didn't have its own in-house employment law team so unfortunately I've had to leave that job behind, but I'm very excited to start something new and I think this firm will be an excellent fit and will allow me to continue my professional development."

(46) In your opinion, what do you think are the three most important characteristics for a lawyer?

Sample answer 1:

"To be a good communicator – solicitors need to be able to explain complicated issues in simple terms, which isn't always an easy thing to do. They also need to have excellent attention to detail. Accuracy is always important, but in the law even a small error can have disastrous consequences. Solicitors also need to have exceptional concentration, as there's a lot of reading and research, which requires very good focus."

Sample answer 2:

"Empathy is an important characteristic, because it enables a lawyer to act in the best interests of their client. Without empathy it's almost impossible to understand a client's position and what matters to them. Self-motivation is another important trait – I think working in the legal profession can be very fast-paced so lawyers need good energy levels and drive. Finally, an ability to get along with people and a sense of humour."

Sample answer 3:

"I think imagination is often an underrated quality in solicitors – certainly when dealing with litigation cases. There will invariably be at least two parties to any dispute, and imagination can help a solicitor get into the mind or minds of their opposite number, helping them to foresee an avenue of attack, or perhaps see a middle way that will bring the case to an amicable close. Passion and enthusiasm are also very important for a lawyer, or anyone working in the legal profession for that matter."

(47) What would you do if you hadn't chosen law?

What are they really asking?

Are you a well-rounded individual with other interests? If you've only ever thought about law and nothing else, that's fine – but you should be able to come up with a hypothetical alternative even if that's the case.

Sample answer 1:

"I always knew I wanted to be a lawyer, but if it wasn't an option then I think I'd have gone into government work. I like the idea of policy-making, or drafting regulations. Something detail-oriented like that would suit me."

Sample answer 2:

"My other passion is history. If I hadn't gone into law, then I might have studied archaeology or palaeontology. I also love writing, so maybe I'd have written history books. I know law was the right choice for me, though."

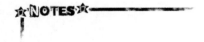 ☆NOTES☆

☆ TOP TIPS ☆

THINKING TIME

If you need a moment to process the question and consider your answer, try not to 'umm' too much. It's perfectly fine to admit that you need a second. You can say: "That's a really interesting question. I'd like to just think about that for a moment." This allows you to take control of the conversation, getting you off the back foot, and suggests that you won't be pushed into a rash answer. Or, if you'd rather give yourself a few extra seconds without umm-ing or admitting that you need more time, you can string out your answer a little by saying: "That's a great question. I don't think I've ever been asked that before. Well, I would have to say, in answer to that, that I believe…" Try not to waffle excessively, but sometimes a little 'talking your way into an answer' gives you a moment to collect your thoughts and may be preferable to a long silence or lots of 'errr'.

☆ NOTES ☆

(48) If you could go back in time, would you still choose to study law?

Answers to avoid

Hint: Don't say no!

Sample answer:

"Yes, definitely, although I might have chosen different electives now that I know what type of law I want to specialise in. I thoroughly enjoyed studying law and I would absolutely make that decision again."

 **☆NOTES☆**

(49) What do you think are the most important qualities in a trainee solicitor?

What are they really asking?

This is a slightly different question from 'What makes a good lawyer', because it's specifically asking about trainees, i.e. you! Answer the question as if they're asking what will make *you* an excellent trainee solicitor.

Sample answer 1:

"*A willingness and ability to learn. Good listening skills. The capacity to accept constructive feedback and put it into practice.*"

Sample answer 2:

"*The ability to get along well with others and be a team player. A professional attitude and a good work ethic. And, of course, an aptitude for law!*"

 ★NOTES★

(50) How would you explain to a client the differences between setting up as a sole trader or a limited company? Give one advantage and one disadvantage for each.

What are they really asking?

They're looking to see how well you explain a concept in simple terms, more so than how detailed your knowledge of the subject is.

Answers to avoid

Don't use too much jargon – the recruiter is assessing how effectively you communicate with a client, so use terms a layperson will understand. Note that the answer below doesn't use phrases such as 'separate legal entity' but instead explains the concept in terms of liability.

Sample answer:

"*I would explain that a sole trader is more exposed to financial risks, because they have unlimited liability for the business and its debts. With a limited company, the client's personal assets aren't at risk, except in certain circumstances, such as a personal guarantee on a business loan. A sole trader pays income tax on their income, whereas a limited company pays corporation tax on its profits. A limited company has shareholders, who effectively own the business but don't run it, and directors, who are responsible for the everyday running and managing of the company. A sole trader is usually one person working alone, although they can have employees. An advantage of being a sole trader is that it's easy to set up and there are fewer filing requirements, so less paperwork. A disadvantage is that raising finance can be more difficult. An advantage of operating as a limited company is that it's generally more tax-efficient, but a disadvantage would be that accounts records and documents are publicly accessible at Companies House and accountancy costs are usually higher.*"

★NOTES★

(51) Which lawyer, real or fictional, do you most admire?

What are they really asking?

The reasons for asking questions like this are partly to see how passionate you are about the law – do you watch legal dramas, read crime fiction, and visit the public gallery of your local court on your day off, for example. Secondly, questions like this can ignite a conversation that gives a glimpse into your personality and interests. That helps the recruiter to gauge how well you're likely to fit in with your potential new colleagues.

Sample answer 1:

"I liked the series Garrow's Law. It's based on the true story of William Garrow, who championed the concept of 'innocent until proven guilty'. He was a pioneer for justice for everyone."

Sample answer 2:

"Baroness Hale. She was the youngest person at the time, and the first female, to be appointed to the Law Commission and she helped create the Children Act 1989. She visited my university once and I found her to be not only inspirational but very passionate about issues that are also important to me."

Sample answer 3:

"Cicero. He was the only Consul of Rome to get to power through sheer force of oratory skill and aptitude for argument. He had no great family, nor military experience or an army behind him, whereas all the other Consuls at the time were military leaders and generals, and came from the state's greatest families. As someone who had to work my way up from a disadvantaged background and poor beginnings, Cicero's always been one of my biggest inspirations. He went from being a nobody to being one of the most important men in the world, for a time, and was voted Father of the Nation."

Sample answer 4:

"A fictional lawyer I really like would have to be Matthew Shardlake in the C. J. Sansom stories. He was a skilled lawyer with a severe disability in an age where that would have presented even more difficulty and impediment than it would now. They're set in Tudor times – have you read any of them?"

Sample answer 5:

"I'm an admirer of Lord Denning. I find him so entertaining and his sense of humour is very like my own. He's also an extremely clever lawyer. I've followed his judgments for a while now."

 ★NOTES★

(52) What is the SRA and what does it do?

What are they really asking?

How much do you know about the profession and how it's regulated?

Answers to avoid

Don't confuse the SRA with the Law Society – they have distinct and different roles within the legal profession. You should be aware of the basic functions and responsibilities of each of these bodies from your Professional Conduct and Regulation studies.

Sample answer:

"The Solicitors Regulation Authority oversees law firms and solicitors in England and Wales. It's responsible for setting professional standards, such as the Code of Conduct, and making sure those principles are upheld. It also provides guidance on ethical issues. When I qualify, I'll need to apply to the SRA to be admitted to the roll of solicitors."

(53) Why do you think law is important to society?

Sample answer:

"Without rules there would be chaos. The law is a framework for what is and is not acceptable in a community. Although the legal system is far from perfect, without the law there would be no protection for victims of dishonesty or other crimes. There would be no certainty in business transactions, and there would be no process or procedure for property ownership or transfer. The law underpins everything that makes a society civilised."

NOTES

iv SKILLS-BASED QUESTIONS

(54) Why do you think you'd be successful in this role?

What are they really asking?

What makes you the best candidate? Give the interviewer a reason (or better still, several reasons) to choose you.

Sample answer:

"I know I'd be successful as a trainee solicitor because I have a quick mind and learn fast. I'm very good with people and get along well with colleagues and clients. Most of all, I'm passionate about building a career in the law and that drive to do well means I'll give my absolute best, all the time. I have an excellent work ethic and always try to go above and beyond what's asked of me."

(55) Can you give an example of a time you had to use your initiative?

What are they really asking?

Will you be able to work without constant supervision after being shown how to do something? Are you a 'self-starter' and able to work independently?

Sample answer 1:

"When I was trying to gain legal work experience, the lockdowns created a big barrier at the start of the pandemic. I came up with the idea of using my office admin experience, but as a freelance service, working from home. I contacted as many local law firms as I could find, offering admin services on a subcontractor basis. One firm responded straight away and gave me a fairly regular stream of transcription work. It gave me some valuable experience at a time when other students' work placements were being cancelled."

Sample answer 2:

"In my current job I'm responsible for dealing with complaints. The company doesn't get many, so it's not something I have to do very often. Unless the amount is significant, I usually try to resolve matters without bothering my manager wherever possible. It's common sense, really – if someone's had a bad experience and a voucher for a free meal is going to retain their custom, I'll make a judgement and issue a compensation voucher. My manager knows that I'll be sensible and use my discretion, so she's happy to let me take the initiative in these situations and deal with it myself."

(56) Give an example of a time when you've handled a situation of disagreement or conflict. What did you do?

What are they really asking?

Are you someone who can listen to others' opinions and resolve conflict assertively?

Sample answer:

"It's not a situation I've found myself in very often, but for part of my law degree I had to give a presentation for a group project. It was a presentation on trusts and one member of the group had misunderstood the distinction between trusts for minors and discretionary trusts. I tried to explain but she was adamant that she was correct and refused to change the script. This person was quite dominating and none of the other students wanted to speak out. I didn't want my grade to suffer because of this, so I printed out the relevant parts of the textbook and highlighted the differences. Just before the next class, I asked her if we could talk. We went outside to a quiet area and I told her I thought that what she had contributed was great, but suggested we tweak the presentation a little. I showed her the printouts and eventually she agreed. It helped that it was just the two of us so perhaps she didn't feel the need to be quite so stubborn without everyone watching."

(57) Give an example of a situation in which you used your skills of persuasion or negotiation. What was the outcome?

Sample answer:

"I was a member of a small committee organising a street party for the Jubilee celebrations. We had to apply to close the street temporarily, and also had to submit a short presentation at a parish meeting. I helped to prepare the presentation and I was selected to field any questions afterwards. Some of the local residents were quite set against the idea of closing the street and having to park their cars elsewhere. I listened to their concerns and explained that the event was only for an afternoon and would be beneficial for the community, but suggested that we implement a driveway-sharing scheme for the day, for people who were unable to walk very far. It was a matter of taking people's comments on board and finding a compromise. The party turned out to be a big success."

☆ TOP TIPS ☆

BUSINESS CARDS

These are extremely cheap to produce now, so consider having a small run of professional 'contact cards' printed and carry a few with you at all times. They don't have to be overly elaborate, just your name and contact details.

(**Extra tip:** set up a professional email which is simply your name, e.g. sarahjanesmith@webmaildomain.net. Keep the quirky email addresses for social use only.)

You never know who you're going to run into, and if you happen to strike up a conversation with a legal recruiter in the supermarket queue, make it easy for them to contact you and give them a card. Don't be afraid to ask for theirs, either!

(58) How do you approach a problem? Can you give a recent example?

What are they really asking?

Problem solving skills are essential for a lawyer. You'll have dealt with problem questions throughout your legal studies, so you can answer this one. The interviewer wants to see if you're a logical planner and can use your initiative.

Sample answer:

"My first step is to analyse all the elements of the problem, including the cause. That helps me form a plan to tackle the problem in the most effective way. In my previous job, I worked for a hotel and had a problem with a double booking. It transpired that there was a glitch in the booking software that counted a booking for two rooms in the same name as one room. I had to contact the software company to resolve that, but the first issue was how to deal with two guests due to arrive and only one room available. There were a few options open to me. I could have called both guests and explained the situation and asked if they were able to change their arrival date, but it was quite late in the day by the time it came to light, so that wasn't very practical. I rang around local hotels, starting with the nearest, and found one with a room of the same type. When the second guest arrived I apologised, explained that I'd moved them to a hotel a few minutes away and called a taxi to take them there, and arranged to pay for their evening meal for the inconvenience. I chose the option that would inconvenience the customer least, by dealing with all the arrangements before they arrived. When tackling any problem, I look at the available options for solutions and identify the one that most effectively resolves the issue."

(59) Give an example of a time you were unsuccessful in handling a situation. What would you do differently if that situation happened again?

What are they really asking?

How do you handle a personal failure? Do you learn from it? Can you admit when you get something wrong?

Answers to avoid

Don't use examples where the consequences were disastrous, or where the reason for the lack of success was down to very poor judgement or recklessness on your part!

Sample answer 1:

"One of my housemates was stealing from the rest of us. I knew it was happening, but because it was just silly little things, I turned a blind eye and didn't say anything. Then money started going missing. I tried to talk to the housemate and see if they needed help, but they got really angry with me and stormed out. It made things really difficult and in the end we all had to move. I should have spoken up sooner. If I was in that situation again, I'd definitely say something as soon as I realised what was happening."

Sample answer 2:

"I work part-time in a pharmacy and I had one customer who was very difficult. He kept insisting his prescription was wrong, and I kept taking it back to the pharmacist, who would send me back out to tell the customer that it was correct. Then he complained because I put the prescription in a bag, shouting at me by this point that he didn't want a bag and hadn't asked for one. He was screaming about the price of prescriptions. In that situation there was very little I could do. I was apologetic, but the customer left still shouting and very angry. Looking back, I realise that the customer was perhaps quite unwell and it really wasn't a personal attack on me."

NOTES

(60) When you're working collaboratively with others, what's your role? Are you usually the leader, a motivator, a quiet observer, an organiser, or something else?

What are they really asking?

What type of team player are you? This is down to personality – there's no right or wrong answer to this question, so just be honest.

Answers to avoid

If you're more of a quiet observer, it's fine to say so, but make sure you highlight your contribution. For example, if you take notes and then summarise for everyone after the initial discussion, make sure you emphasise this. Don't give the impression that you sit back and let others do the work, or that you have nothing to contribute!

Sample answer:

"I'm usually quite good with ideas, so it's often me that starts the discussion off by making suggestions. I tend to be the creative member of the group, and generally I end up in charge of any visual presentations or design element of the project."

 ☆NOTES☆

(61) What would you do if you were given a task that you don't know how to do?

What are they really asking?

This is to measure your problem-solving abilities, and gauge how well you'll cope with the many unfamiliar tasks expected of you as a new lawyer.

Sample answer:

"First, I'd try to use my initiative and work it out, or find a way of researching or looking up what I needed to do, and make sure my work was checked by a supervisor afterwards. If I was still unsure, I'd ask someone to show me what to do. If it's a complicated task with lots of complex steps, I'd make notes so that I had something to follow next time I had to do it."

 ★**NOTES**★

(62) How do you organise your workload when you have several different jobs to complete?

What are they really asking?

Are you good at prioritising and managing your own caseload – crucial for a lawyer!

Sample answer:

"I'm a big fan of lists. Making a 'to do' list helps me to organise and prioritise my tasks into the order in which they need to be done, and ensures anything needing urgent attention is at the top. I usually carry a notebook around so I can jot down reminders for myself, but I also use an organiser app, which sends me alerts when deadlines are approaching. I can also check things off when they're finished and keep track of the work I've done. Just in case technology fails me, I keep a paper list as a backup, too."

(63) You state in your cover letter that you have good time management skills. What techniques do you use to organise your time?

Sample answer:

"*I completed my legal studies while working part-time and running a household. As a result, I've become very good at planning my time carefully so that I could still enjoy my hobbies and see my family and friends. I've always been quite disciplined in that regard. I used a daily planner to set aside time for studying, and stuck to it rigidly, even if it meant I had to miss out on a few events. Planning ahead is the best way to stay organised.*"

☆ TOP TIPS ☆

SELL YOURSELF

This is not the time to be modest. We British are stereotypically self-deprecating and bashful, but the whole point of an interview is to tell the company why you're the best training contract candidate for them. You don't need to over-embellish or exaggerate, and definitely don't lie. Simply have your key USPs (your individual Unique Selling Points) prepared and trot them out at the earliest opportunity! Big yourself up. Don't just say "*I worked in a fast-food restaurant*". Say "*I worked evenings in a fast-food restaurant to fund my college studies, so I've really had to learn to plan and manage my time effectively between my job and studying. It was a very fast-paced, busy city centre venue so I quickly learned to multi-task and work fast but accurately, so that customer service standards were maintained. I also had to handle cash and it was my responsibility to bank large notes regularly.*" SELL IT!

(64) How do you deal with failure? Can you give an example?

What are they really asking?

Are you the sort of person who takes failure to heart? Do you learn from it? Are you emotionally resilient – also a very important trait for an aspiring lawyer!

Sample answer 1:

"*I failed my driving theory test the first time around. I was so disappointed because I really thought I'd done enough and genuinely wasn't expecting to fail. I was annoyed with myself, but when I got home I booked it again for the next available slot, and carried on studying the materials. I passed the second time.*"

Sample answer 2:

"No one likes the idea of failure, but I always try to be a 'get back on the horse' kind of person. Recently, I missed an important appointment. As soon as I realised, I downloaded an organiser app to my phone, so that it wouldn't happen again. I now use it daily and it works well for me."

 **NOTES**

(65) If our fees for a matter are £1,200, how much VAT is payable?

What are they really asking?

It's not a trick question. Most law firms are VAT registered. The current rate of VAT at time of printing is 20%, so it's quite straightforward to calculate for simple round figures. Work out 10% (just remove the last zero, so in this case £120), then double it.

Answers to avoid

Don't panic. If you need some time to work it out, ask the interviewer to give you a moment to think about it. It's better to show that you have the confidence to ask for some thinking time than just give up or say you don't know the answer.

Sample answer:

"20% VAT on £1,200 would be £240."

(66) What is your level of I.T. proficiency?

In this day and age, it should be fairly easy to illustrate several ways in which you use computers or mobile devices to show competence.

Sample answer:

"Very strong. I've always used computers for school and college work and then in my job as admin assistant for the local authority. I'm comfortable with all MS Office programs and I've used book-keeping software. I've also completed a basic coding certificate so I'm fairly computer-savvy."

NOTES

(67) When learning a new, complex task, what's your approach?

What are they really asking?

The recruiter is assessing how you analyse a task, and how methodical and logical your approach is.

Sample answer:

"If I'm shown how to do something new, I'll watch and listen carefully, making notes so that I can refer back later. I'll repeat the task or practise a few times so that the method becomes familiar. I sometimes use mnemonic devices to remember things like steps in a procedure – I found that method extremely useful in answering problem questions in exams, where there was a particular format and order to follow. I think the best way to learn how to do a complex task is to do it as many times as possible until it becomes second nature."

(68) How do you deal with negative feedback?

Sample answer:

"I listen carefully and try to be very open to constructive criticism. Feedback is a highly useful tool for improvement, and I know that starting as a trainee there's going to be a lot for me to learn and take in. I've always read the marker's feedback on my law essays very carefully, and tried to implement it on the next assignment. I don't take negative feedback personally – I value any opportunity to improve and progress in my work."

 ★NOTES★

(69) Have you ever used time recording software? How do you think you would find it?

Sample answer 1:

"Yes, I used to do book-keeping and would use time recording software for my billing systems, so that I knew exactly how much time I'd spent on each customer's work and had a record. I found it invaluable. I would have no problems using something similar to record the time I spend on each file as a trainee solicitor."

Sample answer 2:

"I haven't had the opportunity to use time recording software yet, but I'm a very quick learner, especially with computer software. I can see how it would be invaluable for accurate client billing and I'm sure I wouldn't have any difficulty getting to grips with it."

v COMMERCIAL AWARENESS QUESTIONS

Many law students are either mystified or terrified by the idea of commercial awareness questions. There's nothing to worry about and the questions are not actually difficult to answer, with a little bit of forward planning. Commercial awareness questions are designed to assess your awareness and appreciation of key commercial factors that a typical business should consider. Your answers should demonstrate both commercial understanding and common sense.

Follow the news headlines, especially in the days and weeks leading up to your interview. Pick out stories that may have a legal angle in terms of business law, public law, or employment law, for example. Think about how the law you've studied fits in with these events. Some examples from recent history might be the P&O Ferries controversy, the Post Office accounting software scandal and of course the many and nebulous effects of the COVID-19 pandemic.

(70) What do you think are the main problems/opportunities facing the legal profession today?

What are they really asking?

This question is asked to see how well you understand the concept of the law firm as a business. All firms are affected by regulatory matters, the global business and financial environment, political issues and technological trends, to name but a few examples. Show that you understand this by focusing on one or two intelligent observations.

Sample answer:

"I've seen that, like many businesses, several law firms in this practice area have been affected by sanctions in Russia and had to close their operations. This will have a huge impact on the business and the staff, but they're now expanding their operations into other countries, which could be an exciting new opportunity. I've also noted that ABC Law Firm and XYZ Law Ltd have adopted a trial model of a staggered four-day working week. It will be interesting to see how client care and productivity are affected and how that balances with staff well-being. Most firms coped very well with staff absences, lockdowns and working from home during the pandemic, and I think technology has made the legal industry a lot more adaptable than perhaps it once was."

NOTES

(71) To what extent do you think legislation should play a role in reducing carbon emissions?

What are they really asking?

Think of these questions as your conclusion to a short essay question. Your ability to articulate a point of view is more important than the actual opinion. Sum up your main points, be concise and be persuasive.

Answers to avoid

Don't sit on the fence – pick a side and give an intelligent reason.

Sample answer 1:

"*Although I appreciate that there has to be some limitation on state interference in the lives of individuals and businesses, the status quo is insufficient in terms of any meaningful reduction in carbon emissions. Not enough is being done and if the only way to achieve a result is by imposing legal obligations, restrictions and penalties then I believe that's a sacrifice of certain liberties that's worth making. Environmental damage is not something about which we have the luxury of waiting around and hoping for the best. Action is needed and legislation is one tool with which to take that action and make a positive change. Much greater consequences for the biggest offenders are needed if any real difference is to be made.*"

Sample answer 2:

"*Reducing carbon emissions is of extremely high importance, and I don't feel that enough is being done globally to resolve this problem. However, legislation isn't the answer. The biggest culprits are unlikely to be swayed by the prospect of a fine or even a custodial sentence, and in any case such penalties would be all but impossible to enforce. The problem is worldwide and needs to be tackled through education and improvements in energy technology. Historically the law isn't terribly effective in tackling this type of issue. The low number of prosecutions under the Corporate Manslaughter Act is evidence of that.*"

(72) What changes do you think the legal world will have to adapt to post-pandemic?

Sample answer:

"Several changes have come about that will affect most businesses, such as the prevalence of hybrid working and the increase in work-from-home arrangements and employees' expectations in that regard. There are also changes in legislation, such as the law on commercial rent arrears, which lawyers will need to keep abreast of. I've read that there are even cases being brought now under disability discrimination legislation on behalf of people suffering from long Covid. I do think that it's also created opportunities for the legal profession as a result, though. For example, it's made many people consider the need for estate planning."

☆ TOP TIPS ☆
CONTACTING THE COMPANY

In correspondence with a legal recruiter, mirror both their tone and method of contact. If they email you, email back. If they phone, phone back. It's NEVER acceptable to reply to a phone call with a text message. Reflect their tone and style. This may sound obvious, and it's basic business etiquette, but if they write to you with a 'Dear Mr Evans' and a 'Kind regards', don't respond with 'Hiya Mike' and 'Cheers'.

(73) Tell me about a recent legal development that caught your interest.

What are they really asking?

Are you on top of current events and do you follow updates in the law? It's very easy to stay informed about legal matters – subscribe to sites such as Lexology or the Law Society Gazette for daily digests in your chosen areas of law. That way, you can easily have a few hot topics up your sleeve ready to whip out at a moment's notice!

Answers to avoid

Here's a simple tip to remember. When referring to a recent item of legal news, avoid saying "I heard..." or (worse) "I saw on Facebook..." and say "I read..." instead.

Sample answer 1:

"I'm following the progress of the Renters' Reform Bill with interest as I've personally found it difficult to find a suitable rental property that will accept pets. I think it's a very positive development and will make a lot of people's lives easier. Ending no-fault evictions will give a lot more security and protection to people who are renting."

Sample answer 2:

"I've been reading a lot about ESG recently [you may need to explain what this is – take the cue from your interviewer and if they aren't nodding in clear understanding, tell them what the letters stand for!] *– that's environmental, social and governance criteria in investments. There have been many reports of 'greenwashing', where companies have exaggerated the green credentials of their investments. I'm actually using ESG as the topic for my LLM dissertation, so I've been following these articles very closely and it's been quite eye-opening. It's a very new issue, but with an emerging generation of millennial investors I think it's going to become very important in corporate finance law, which I hope will be one of my training seats here, if I am successful."*

NOTES

125

(74) What impact do you think the EU Withdrawal Act has had in the UK and abroad?

What are they really asking?

They're not asking about your political leanings (and they're not allowed to!) – this is more about assessing your understanding of global legal developments. Keep your answer intelligent, factual and as neutral as possible, and try to keep personal political opinion out. You can have a good debate when you've bagged the job, but the training contract interview isn't the place to soapbox.

Sample answer:

"There's been an impact on a vast number of areas, many of which still need to be addressed so there's still some uncertainty in areas such as copyright law and finance. The main impact is constitutional – the whole constitution of the UK is now very different, even though much of the EU legislation previously adopted will remain. The limitations on free movement of people is a very controversial issue, but globally I'd say that the biggest impact is on trade. For trading within Europe there are now more barriers to overcome than when the UK was a Member State, and this seems to have caused some very costly delays to the supply and transport of goods. I'm hopeful that these issues will be ironed out in time and that businesses can continue to export without too much extra hindrance, because that affects the whole economy."

127

(75) Can you think of a recent development in our area of legal specialism? Why is it important?

What are they really asking?

By the time you get to interview you will, of course, have researched the company carefully and you'll know exactly what type of work they do. This is just a narrowing-down of the subject and should be easy to have ready if you prepare a little in advance.

Sample answer 1:

"I hope to work in international finance law for one of my training seats, and one of the topics I've been reading a lot about recently is the law on electronic signatures. There have been quite a few developments in this area and I think it will help to speed things up for companies dealing across borders. The scope for fraud or error is much smaller than it was when this technology was first introduced. I wrote my dissertation on legal tech and in the last few years, technology such as smart contracts has really progressed quickly. It's going to be very important for future lawyers to keep on top of technological developments."

Sample answer 2:

"I've read that ground rents have been abolished for new leases from June 2022, which is quite a big development for property lawyers and conveyancers. The fines for breaching this legislation are quite significant, too, so developers will have to be very carefully advised."

Sample answer 3:

"The new application process for divorce seems a lot more straightforward than the previous route. I think the availability of no-fault divorce will make things a little less painful for separating couples, especially those with a family who want to keep things amicable and as civil as possible."

(76) If you were advising a client who wanted to open a restaurant, what would you encourage them to consider? What other advice might you give?

What are they really asking?

You may encounter a variation on this question if the firm you're applying to carries out different types of work. For example, if you're applying to a small high street firm that does mostly conveyancing, you might be asked what advice you'd give to someone buying a property locally. Expect follow-up questions as your interviewer may want to hone in on aspects of your answer. They may ask you to go into more detail about setting up a partnership, for example, or to explain how a SWOT analysis works.

Sample answer:

"I think the first thing to consider would be what form to set up as, and explain the pros and cons of setting up as a limited company or a partnership. Then I'd discuss financing the business, and see if they have a business plan with a cash flow forecast that we could discuss. We'd need to consider employer's responsibilities and health and safety requirements. Then there's the restaurant itself – are they purchasing a property or renting premises? Does that need finance, will renovations need to be made, is the location and parking suitable, and so on. Other than legal advice, I'd also ask them about plans for marketing and promotion, gather information on their relevant experience and background, and make sure they're fully prepared and equipped for starting a business. They'll need to consider the long hours, difficulty in taking holidays, and what would happen if they fell ill, for example. Staffing can also be very difficult in the catering industry as turnover tends to be high, and good chefs are particularly hard to come by."

NOTES

(77) What recent legal decision do you particularly agree or disagree with? And why?

What are they really asking?

This is less about your opinion and more about how you articulate your arguments for or against the decision. You can be as passionate as you like, as long as you're persuasive and eloquent! Be ready for follow-up questions with this type of interviewing.

Sample answer 1:

"I personally agreed with the recent ruling that business insurers must pay out under policies that covered against closure due to infectious diseases. In most cases the wording was very clear and it was unreasonable for the insurers to claim any other interpretation. I've seen first-hand how small businesses in particular were affected by the lockdowns, and denying their claims was simply unjust."

Sample answer 2:

"I disagree with the decision to overturn Roe v Wade in the USA. I feel quite strongly that this shouldn't even have been considered, as it seems like a big step backwards for women's rights. I appreciate that some people are very strongly anti-abortion, but they're not personally affected by someone else's choices. I'm a passionate believer in retaining that freedom to choose."

(78) What qualities make a good manager?

What are they really asking?

Many firms interview with one eye on future partner potential. If you're asked this question, take it as a positive sign!

Sample answer:

"A good manager is one who leads by example. I had one supervisor at my last job who made a point of not asking anyone to do anything they weren't willing to do themselves, and she would frequently jump on the phones when it was busy, or clean the staff kitchen, and she got a lot of respect for mucking in. Managing a team needs very good people skills – strong communication, and being assertive rather than aggressive when dealing with staff. Compassion is also a very important trait in a manager. They need to be dedicated, too, because there will often be extra responsibilities and expectations, such as longer hours, in a management position, so they need to be quite resilient and energetic."

 ☆NOTES☆

(79) What do you think are the three most important ingredients for a successful business?

Sample answer:

"I think the most important factor for any business is its people. You could have the best product in the world but if the people behind it are no good, it will fail. A successful business needs a strong team. A great product or service that people want or need is essential. Finally, a way to promote that product or service. If nobody knows about it, it won't sell, so a successful business also needs good marketing."

(80) What changes would you make to current company law?

What are they really asking?

This type of question is designed to distinguish between those who can reel off memorised information, and those who can think critically about a topic and analyse it intelligently. The key with questions like this is to not over-think it. Ask yourself what you know about the subject. You can usually find an angle – there's no need to try to bluff.

Sample answer:

"From a legal perspective, I would introduce a distinction between large and small companies. As things currently stand, small businesses are subject to the same reporting requirements, the same taxation and the same regulation as large international corporations, and it seems unbalanced. Larger companies often pay less tax than small businesses because they're in a better position to exploit accountancy loopholes, or invest in other assets, which they then also profit from. Smaller businesses tend not to have these advantages. I'd give small and start-up businesses a better rate of corporation tax based on number of employees and annual turnover. Helping a business get off the ground is the best way to build that business into a successful one, and therefore one that actually pays more tax in its following years."

★ TOP TIPS ★

ONLINE PRESENCE

If you're on social media, check your account and make sure there's nothing on there that you wouldn't want a potential employer to see. Recruiters will look you up online so go through everything and delete anything that might go against you as a training contract candidate. Before posting anything, think: would I want my future employer to read this? If the answer is no, just don't post it. Remember that comments you leave on other people's posts are also visible.

(81) Which newspapers do you read?

What are they really asking?

A sneaky interviewer may use this question to try to gauge your political leanings (which they're not allowed to ask about, incidentally). Or they may just be interested in how connected you are with current events, whether you follow legal and societal developments closely and whether you're someone who likes to stay informed.

Answers to avoid

Don't say 'I don't really follow the news' – this may come across as uninterested and even ill-informed. Try to avoid naming tabloids as your source of news. Snobbish or not, there's an expectation of lawyers to read the broadsheets for their news rather than the red-tops.

Sample answer:

"I tend to follow the news online now rather than buy papers, so I get a good mix of views from different news outlets. I also subscribe to the Law Society Gazette for my legal news."

(82) Who are our main competitors?

What are they really asking?

This question is asked to find out if you've done your research – not only into the firm you're interviewing at, but into the associated legal landscape as well. If you've done your homework, you'll have a couple of names ready, and your answer to this doesn't need to be long.

Sample answer:

"*I would say that the closest firm geographically is Shardlake's Law – they cover similar areas of law but they don't do any criminal work. There's also Hadrian's Law over in Wallsland, which is a slightly smaller company but also offers similar services.*"

 NOTES

(83) Can you name any of our major corporate clients?

What are they really asking?

Also an easy one to have ready. For smaller firms this is less likely to be relevant (and so you probably won't be asked). Client confidentiality means that you probably won't be able to look up who the local conveyancing firm bought property for! For corporate firms, though, you'll usually find success stories on their websites, naming their important clients.

Sample answer:

"I'm aware that you acted for Tyrannosaur Tech in their takeover of Cretaceous Global recently, and that the negotiations took place over about eight months. I'd love to ask you about how the staff approached that challenge if we have time at the end?"

 ☆NOTES☆

(84) What do you think the long-term impact of COVID-19 will be for commercial property law?

What are they really asking?

Whether you're able to put into perspective the legal aspects of a social issue.

Sample answer:

"I think it's fair to say that, firstly, there will be a lasting impact on the demand for commercial property as more people adapt to working from home and shopping online, so developers and commercial landlords may be detrimentally affected. The legislation that was introduced during the pandemic also temporarily suspended the rights of commercial property owners to determine leases or bring actions for rent arrears. Although I believe this legislation has now come to an end, it's going to take some businesses a long time to recover, and many have folded during the lockdowns, so landlords are left unable to recover the rent owed at all. I expect that commercial property owners will be more wary as a result and may want to incorporate stricter payment clauses into new leases."

★NOTES★

(85) What is your leadership style and why do you think this works?

What are they really asking?

It's unlikely you'll be asked this question unless you have some previous leadership experience, but for career changers the interviewer may want to gauge whether you might be suited to a more supervisory role once you've finished your training contract.

Answers to avoid

Don't say that you've never really been a leader. Think back. Group projects at university that you managed? Captain of a sports team? Give an example if you can.

Sample answer 1:

"I've always been a good communicator, so I'd say my leadership style is primarily about facilitating communication. I try to encourage people and bring out their strengths. In my last job, I had one member of the team who hated answering the phone and would always try to avoid it. We worked together on his telephone skills and even did some role-playing scenarios to work through his 'nightmare customer' fears. He went on to become one of the strongest call handlers on the team."

Sample answer 2:

"I lead by example. I like to show people my methods and demonstrate exactly what's expected, rather than just tell them. I think this works because people's expectations are managed, and they tend to reflect the behaviour they see around them. If I'm positive, communicative and respectful, I usually find that my staff reciprocate and we have a happy, relaxed workplace."

Sample answer 3:

"I'm good at spotting where others excel, so I can delegate very effectively. I was in charge of a group project at uni where we had to mock up a criminal trial. I put the most confident and outspoken member of the group

as lead counsel, and selected a fairly quiet member of the group as the judge, because I knew that even though she was softly spoken, she was very shrewd and would do a great job of the judgment. I allocated all the roles within the group and I think I judged it well. I can usually spot strong points in people, even if they're not aware of them themselves."

 ★NOTES★

144

vi TRICKY QUESTIONS

(Designed to test your ability to deal with
unexpected or tricky issues.)

**(86) If you could have dinner with any three people from history, who
would you choose and why?**

What are they really asking?

There's no right or wrong answer to this type of question, so don't
over-think it, but it's the sort of question you can prepare for in advance.
The interviewer wants to hear your reasons, so it's a good idea to
pick people who reflect your character – a sportsperson if you have
an interest in sports, a musician you admire or someone from history
who accomplished great things. Marie Curie, Johnny Cash, Elizabeth I,
Professor Brian Cox, Raksha Dave and Oskar Schindler were all great
examples given by candidates who were able to explain their choices with
an interesting reason.

Answers to avoid

Try to avoid naming a celebrity and saying 'because I just like them'.
Choosing a varied mix of modern and historical, male and female
characters shows a good range of knowledge and suggests that you can
interact with people from different backgrounds and walks of life.

Don't feel that you have to tie every answer to the law. If you're a fan of Horace Rumpole (aren't we all?) or Harvey Specter, then by all means say so, but this is more about *why* you picked these people than who you chose. What qualities do they possess that make you want to be in their company? What does it say about you?

Sample answer:

"I would pick comedian Richard Ayoade because he'd keep everyone entertained and I really like his style of humour, Boadicea because she had such an interesting, if brutal, life and I'm fascinated by that period of history, and George Stephenson – I'd ask him what he thought about the Beeching report!"

☆ TOP TIPS ☆

BAG IT UP!

Carry a smart bag or briefcase to hold copies of your CV, a copy of this book (for last-minute swotting), some mints, emergency deodorant, a pen and your wallet or purse. It doesn't need to be expensive, just businesslike. Again, this may sound obvious, even a little old-fashioned, but a smart, professional appearance will enhance your interviewer's impression of how serious you are about joining them.

Some form of attaché case *vs* a carrier bag. No brainer.

(87) What is the last book you read that wasn't a law textbook?

What are they really asking?

What we choose to read can say a lot about who we are, but this is more about *how* you answer the question – and of course, whether you read in your spare time. It doesn't really matter what you read. If you can find something interesting or positive to say about the book, so much the better.

Answers to avoid

'I don't really read' would be a bad answer, but even worse would be to start rattling off titles of all the classics you can remember, but haven't actually read. If your interviewer happens to be a big fan of Dickens and starts asking follow-up questions, you're going to come unstuck.

Sample answer:

"It's been a while since I was able to read anything other than my LPC books, but when the exams finished, I dug out an Asimov collection of short stories I've loved since I was a child. I'm quite a big science fiction fan, and that wasn't too heavy-going after all the studying. I really like George Orwell too, and my guilty pleasure is the Harry Potter series."

(88) What is the biggest mistake you've ever made?

What are they really asking?

This question is really asking how you deal with your own mistakes. Do you recognise them, correct them and learn from them? Can you turn mistakes into opportunities? Do you repeat the same patterns? Have an answer prepared that shows how you confronted a mistake and dealt with it. Perhaps you regret not studying law earlier, or maybe you ended up in a career that wasn't right for you. Demonstrate how you overcame these issues.

Answers to avoid

Avoid giving examples where you did something silly through pure youthful foolishness, and avoid examples where the consequences were dire. Recognising your own errors is part of growth, but don't paint yourself in a bad light unnecessarily.

Sample answer:

"I followed my parents' career path – they were both teachers and it was always assumed I'd go into teaching as well. I enjoyed aspects of the job, but it just wasn't for me. It was a mistake not to choose my own path and I wish I'd taken different subjects and gone straight into law. On the other hand, though, teaching equipped me with some very useful transferable skills and valuable experience, which I'm sure will come in very useful as a trainee solicitor. I don't think any experience is ever wasted."

(89) Would you ever bend the rules if the situation justified it?

What are they really asking?

Situational judgement questions such as these are not uncommon in training contract interviews. You may be given more specific detail, or a hypothetical situation, and asked how you'd deal with it. They're not designed to trick you and there's no right or wrong answer *per se*. Be honest and logical in your answer.

Sample answer:

"It depends on the situation. If, for example, I saw someone in trouble in a lake, but there was a sign saying 'Private – No Entry', then in those circumstances I'd ignore the sign and try to help the person. Generally, though, I do follow the rules and there would have to be a good reason for me to deliberately flout them."

(90) If you were a biscuit, what sort of biscuit would you be?

What are they really asking?

This type of question may come up in many forms. Some interviewers like to throw in an obscure question such as 'If you could have one superpower, what would it be?' or 'If you had a theme tune that played whenever you walked into a room, what song would it be?' On the surface, these questions serve no obvious purpose, and many candidates struggle to give a structured, well-considered answer to such a seemingly absurd question. The interviewer is ostensibly evaluating your ability to 'think on your feet', but in reality, this type of bizarre questioning is somewhat out of place in the legal profession. It does happen, though, so be ready.

Answers to avoid

A peeved candidate replied to one such question by saying, 'Ask me something else that's actually related to the job.' The irritation is understandable, but the attitude cost them a second interview. Even if you find these questions exasperating, try to answer them and direct the conversation back to your skills and strengths.

Sample answer:

"I would say a shortbread biscuit – it's unique and doesn't melt or crumble. I think that reflects my ability to keep it together in high pressure situations. Would you like me to give an example of that?"

NOTES

(91) Have you ever attended court or a tribunal?

What are they really asking?

Questions like this are designed to set apart those candidates who have a genuine interest in the legal profession. The more you can demonstrate a passion for law, the better your chances of making the shortlist for a training contract.

Sample answer 1:

"I had to attend court as part of a family matter several years ago, and it was that process that really got me interested in law. I found it so interesting I decided to take an introductory law course, and that's how I got started on this path. I decided I wanted to help families who were in the same position I was in a few years ago."

Sample answer 2:

"At college we had several day trips to different courts. My favourite was the Royal Courts of Justice in London. It was fascinating to see a real trial in progress and I was hooked on criminal law from that day. Since then, I've visited four times on my own, whenever I've had the chance."

(92) If you felt that one of your colleagues was making a lot of mistakes, what would you do?

Sample answer:

"If it was appropriate for me to do so, I'd talk to them first and see if there was anything going on that they may need help with. A colleague in my last job started making a lot of mistakes, which was very out of character, and it transpired that she hadn't told us her brother was dying. My first reaction would be to see if there was anything I could do to help. As a trainee solicitor, though, my authority over another member of the team would probably be quite limited so the next option would be to mention anything specific to human resources so that they could look at any extra training needs. I'd try to avoid pointing out their errors in front of anyone or humiliating them."

(93) What's your favourite colour?

What are they really asking?

There's a somewhat old-fashioned school of thought that a person's favourite colour provides a unique insight into their psyche. Psychologically, a person whose favourite colour is red, for example, is said to possess strong energy and power. Blue is a calm, peaceful persona. And so on. This is another of those 'What sort of biscuit are you?' questions that are (thankfully) falling into the annals of history, but occasionally they do make an appearance in training contract interviews.

Answers to avoid

Black. Colour theory psychology suggests that those who prefer black are gloomy and malevolent(!) As ridiculous as that may sound, being able to think on your feet when presented with a preposterous question will earn you interview points, so answer as sensibly as you can and try to move the conversation along to more relevant topics.

Sample answer:

"I don't really have one favourite colour, and my home décor is fairly neutral, but aesthetically I tend to go for blues and yellows, as blue is calm and peaceful and yellow is cheerful. I'd say that I'm a calm person and I do try to remain cheerful in the middle of a crisis. I can give you an example of that if you'd like me to?"

(94) During your training contract, you're observing a meeting between a senior partner and a long-standing client. The partner gives incorrect legal advice to the client. What do you do?

Sample answer:

"I'd try to avoid saying anything in front of the client, but I'd ask the senior partner to clarify the point for me after the meeting, in case I'd simply misunderstood something. It would be easier in a private conversation to explain my understanding of the matter and make sure the client had been given the correct information."

 ☆NOTES☆

158

(95) What is your worst habit?

Answers to avoid

Try to pick something fairly innocuous that they're unlikely to be too irritated by. Don't say 'I work too hard' – it sounds false and a bit pretentious. You're human, and so is everyone else who works there. Be yourself.

Sample answer 1:

"I have a bad habit of 'talking with my hands'. I'm trying to keep them in my lap now so that I'm not waving them around, but when I'm enthused or if I'm explaining something I do tend to gesticulate."

Sample answer 2:

"My worst habit at school and college was not speaking up when I knew the answer. It was very different in uni, though, and I stopped feeling so self-conscious about it. Now I always speak up."

★ TOP TIPS ★
! FORBIDDEN TERRITORY !

Things prospective employers are not allowed to ask you about: your age; your sexual orientation; your religion; marital status; children and family plans – this list is by no means exhaustive. Interviewers can ask about your health and any disabilities, but they cannot discriminate against you for it. Most law firms know enough about employment law not to venture into these areas, but it does happen occasionally. If you're asked about these areas, it's up to you whether you choose to answer, and whether you continue the interview.

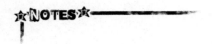

NOTES

(96) You're working on a very important case with an urgent deadline. By the end of the working day, it's still not ready and needs another hour of work to finish off. What do you do?

What are they really asking?

How are your self-management skills? Are you willing to put in extra time and effort when needed?

Answers to avoid

Expectations of trainee solicitors are much higher than in other jobs, especially in larger corporate firms. If you're unwilling to go beyond the 9 to 5 you've probably picked the wrong career!

Sample answer:

"I appreciate that sometimes flexibility is required of a trainee solicitor, and I know that a training contract is not a 'clock-in-clock-out' 9 to 5 role. I'd just get myself an extra coffee and push on. If there's one thing I learned as a law student it's the importance of deadlines, and I'm very disciplined about submitting work on time. It wouldn't sit well with me to just walk away and miss the target. I'd have to just get it done."

(97) What would you do if you made a mistake that impacted a client?

What are they really asking?

A recruiter wants to know if a candidate is going to be honest and hold their hands up when they get something wrong – which everyone does at some point. If it happens, don't be afraid to tell your supervising solicitor, but tell them *quickly*.

Sample answer:

"I'd have to own up as soon as I realised, so that the company could mitigate as quickly as possible, if necessary. I'd tell my supervising solicitor what had happened and try to help put things right. I wouldn't try to cover things up, and I wouldn't try to fix a big mistake without telling anyone, although I'd be trying to find a solution. I'm a very meticulous person by nature, and make every conscious effort not to make mistakes, but I accept that everyone is human and sometimes it does happen."

NOTES

(98) Can you give an example of an obstacle you've overcome?

Answers to avoid

It may be that you consider yourself quite fortunate and you haven't faced any major obstacles. That's fine, but see if you can think of any examples where you've faced a challenge. Perhaps a difficult situation in a previous job, or moving to a new area, or you've battled with a hidden disability. All these things are examples of some form of obstacle.

Sample answer:

"My background was not a privileged one, so I had no contacts or connections in the legal profession and no real guidance. I was the first in my family to attend university, and without the advantages of knowing anyone in the business I had to make my own opportunities. I gained experience by volunteering at the university law centre and that helped me to meet people in the law who were happy to share their insight into the profession. I had to put myself right out of my comfort zone and build a network from scratch, but I'm quite proud that I managed to do that without any kind of head-start."

★NOTES★

(99) Which of your previous jobs did you enjoy least, and why?

What are they really asking?

It's important to know what aspects of a job you find least enjoyable, so that your training plan can not only reflect your strengths but also work on areas that need improvement. It's equally important to find out if someone has aversions to certain tasks that might make them unsuitable for the position. This is one of those questions where it helps to be able to turn negatives into positives.

Answers to avoid

One candidate declared that they hated their job in retail because they 'couldn't stand dealing with the public'. Suffice to say, they didn't get the training contract. Solicitors' clients are, more often than not, members of the public!

Sample answer:

"I took a summer labouring job on a building site in my first year of university. It was hard physical work, which I didn't mind at all, but it wasn't a very interesting job as there was no real mental stimulation or challenge. I was just pushing wheelbarrows around and moving bags of plaster. It was difficult not to be bored, and I really craved something more intellectually demanding. The following summer I worked for the same company but in the accounts office, which was more interesting and I really enjoyed it."

(100) What salary are you looking for?

What are they really asking?

This is in the 'Tricky Questions' category because it sometimes requires careful navigation. Training contract salaries are usually stated clearly in the advertisement, and starting rates are fairly standard across the board (with London usually slightly higher). However, if the salary hasn't been disclosed and you're asked what you're looking for, be aware that the range for first-year trainee solicitors is usually around £20-22k outside London. London firms can be anywhere from £20k-50k as a starting wage. The Law Society's recommended minimum salary for trainees is currently (at time of printing) £22,794 in London and £20,217 outside London.

Sample answer:

"I know that I'll be starting at trainee level and that there's a generally accepted salary range. I do feel that I'd be bringing several years of experience in business to the role, and ideally, I'm looking for somewhere between £X and £X. I'm very interested in the role and keen to get started in the profession – that's my main priority rather than salary, so I'm open to talking further about the details if I'm successful today."

Where your personal '£X' and '£X' lie is for you to determine, but have a figure in mind and be able to justify it. Giving a range also leaves room for negotiation if you're successful in the interview.

(101) If you could give your teenage self one piece of advice, what would it be?

What are they really asking?

An insight into who you are, and your personal 'back story'. Everyone wishes they'd done something differently at some point – be honest.

Sample answer 1:

"I'd tell myself to study law at 18 instead of going into hospitality. I didn't have the self-belief to realise I could become a lawyer. My advice to younger me would be to have more confidence in my abilities and do what I really wanted to do."

Sample answer 2:

"My advice to any teenager – including myself – would be to trust my own instincts and not listen to negative people who try to talk you out of going for opportunities. I had a friend who tried to convince me not to become a lawyer, and now I realise that came from jealousy. Never listen to the naysayers!"

NOTES

TIPS FOR STUDENTS

Most training contract candidates are likely to be students. Some may have already completed the LPC and some may still be finishing their degree or conversion course. It's to be expected that students probably won't have a vast amount of legal work experience, but that doesn't matter. You can use academic experiences to answer most of the work-related questions in this book.

If you're really struggling to find examples, you can always give a hypothetical answer to a hypothetical scenario. Try to avoid doing so repeatedly, but if you're genuinely stuck on a question, you can say something along the lines of: "*I haven't really experienced that type of situation yet, but what I'd probably do in those circumstances is...*"

Don't underestimate the value of your educational experience. You've shown resilience in completing a very tough degree, and you've demonstrated that you can prioritise deadlines, manage your own time and work under pressure. A law degree takes self-motivation, determination and drive to succeed – all excellent qualities and essential for an aspiring lawyer. If you've participated in group projects or extracurricular activities, even experiences such as travelling, you have a wealth of experience to draw from – don't be afraid to use it.

Example: *"My degree has given me a great deal of experience in managing my time, researching solutions to problems, working with others, organising my own workload and finding information. These skills are imperative for a lawyer and I'm keen to use them as a trainee solicitor."*

Many students have part-time jobs during university, often in hospitality, food service or retail. Employers love candidates with this type of experience, because the work is usually very fast-paced in a high-pressure environment, meaning students who have worked in these jobs are able to multitask, think on their feet and work quickly and efficiently. This experience will stand you in very good stead for a role in the legal profession.

If you've volunteered at a law clinic or served on any student committee, this is also a great advantage when it comes to training contract applications. You can demonstrate that you can work in a team, and you're organised and disciplined.

The biggest mistake students tend to make is playing down their very valuable experiences because they're 'only bar work' or 'just voluntary work' or 'only a uni project' – these experiences are extremely attractive to employers so don't dismiss the skills they've given you. Use them!

Tips for Career Changers

Career changers have a wealth of transferable skills, knowledge and life experience to draw from, so don't ever feel disadvantaged just because you've taken a less conventional route into law. It can be very attractive to an employer.

If you're a mature candidate, your age is not against you. It can be an advantage. On your CV and application forms you're not obliged to give your age, and prospective employers cannot ask, but there's nothing stopping you from working it into the conversation at interview if you choose to do so. As someone with work experience, you can jump in and hit the ground running. Conversely, some firms may be looking for trainees they can mould and shape, in which case being 21 and brand new to the profession may take the edge. It's horses for courses – you decide if it's appropriate to highlight your previous life experience.

In the interview, focus on the skills you've honed in your current career. Strong communication, problem solving, leadership experience and customer service are all extremely relevant and highly valuable to a legal recruiter, so speak up and let them know your capabilities.

You can prepare examples to commonly asked questions based on your working life to date. Use the sample questions above to prepare skeleton answers to the topics that are most likely to come up, and you can rattle these off without hesitation in the interview.

★ NOTES ★

PERSONALITY TESTS

Also referred to as psychometric tests or aptitude tests, personality tests can take several forms. Often, the questions won't appear to relate to the job role, and can be as exasperating as the 'What sort of biscuit are you?' type of question.

There are no right or wrong (or obvious) answers, which can be frustrating to a logical legal mind, but the key is to try not to over-think it. Generally, you're expected to simply choose the answer that most appeals to you at first glance without hesitating or thinking too much about what the question is really asking.

You can – and should – prepare for this type of test. There are numerous free resources online where you can take practice tests and receive feedback on your answers. The more you practise, the easier you'll find the real thing, and the more you'll get to know the type of question and the most appropriate answer for you. Some of the questions may even seem ridiculous, or may not supply an answer that would fit your behaviour, so the quicker you learn to dispatch such questions without dwelling on which 'wrong' answer you should pick, the more prepared you'll be for this type of test should one come up. Practise.

Competency-based interviews don't focus on your interests, your educational accomplishments or your work experience. They're purely about skills and abilities. You'll need to prepare plenty of examples (Hint: use the Skills question templates above) because most of the questions will ask you to demonstrate a time when you've displayed a particular trait. For example, you may be asked to describe an occasion where you've utilised your skills of persuasion; flexibility and adaptability; teamwork; problem solving; leadership; time management; initiative; decision making; and so on. Have those examples ready before the interview and you'll fly through it.

CONFIDENCE BUILDING

The key to interview confidence is to practise. Practise, practise, practise. Use the sample questions and template answers in this book to prepare your own answers and rehearse the structure of your response. Don't try to learn answers verbatim, like a script, because it will come across as unnatural, but try to commit the main bullet points to memory so that you have a 'road map' of potential answers ready in your head.

If your university has a careers department, they may offer interview coaching and mock interviews. This can feel very nerve-wracking but do make use of the opportunity. It's better to get the scary part out of the way in a pretend scenario, so that by the time the real interview comes around it's not so new and terrifying! They may also pick up any weaknesses in your technique, so you can nip them in the bud.

Ask friends or family to 'interview' you, using the questions in this book as a framework, and practise your responses. This will give you the chance to both refine your answers and tackle any nervous habits like twirling your hair or jiggling your legs. If you're brave enough, video it and watch it back so that you can also look out for negative body language (folded arms, frowning, slouching, lack of eye contact).

A good confidence-building technique is to write down all the things you're good at, your successes, and things that are unique about you. Not only will this give your self-esteem a boost, it will also codify your personal 'selling points' in your own mind, ready for you to talk about them with self-assurance in the interview.

 NOTES

HOW TO HANDLE CAREER
GAPS OR WEAK POINTS

If there are gaps in your CV, it's best to be honest and explain them. Find the positives – what did you learn, accomplish or experience in any non-working time? If you took a career break to go travelling or have children, if you were ill or were simply between jobs for a while, it's fine to say so – and you're certainly not alone. Briefly explain the reasons for any gaps, preferably with a few examples of anything positive that you did during that period; you don't need to go into lots of detail.

If you've been ill, or perhaps caring for a sick relative, explain why you feel you're now ready to return to work, and focus on why you'd be a great fit for the trainee position. Perhaps the experience made you stronger, more caring or gave you useful experience? There will almost always be something you can use positively.

Have you travelled? This will have given you a wonderful insight and experience of other cultures, and demonstrates independence and initiative, so talk about it. Where did you go? What did you learn? What skills did you utilise?

Perhaps you went back to education as a career changer. Again, this shows courage and determination, so focus on how you arrived at the decision to start something new, how you managed your time and how you balanced a home life with university studies.

Changing jobs several times in a short space of time can also raise questions, so be ready with your reasons. Be sure to state what's different now – the interviewer will be keen to know what's changed, to reassure them that you won't be looking to leave the job after a few months if they've invested in training you. Many of us have had jobs that just weren't a good fit, but use the sample answers above to craft a positive answer. There's no shame in moving on from an unfulfilling job if a better opportunity presents itself.

Redundancy is a common reason for career gaps, and there's no reason to see this as a negative factor in the interview. Explain how you used your time when your job was made redundant. Give examples of your performance and accomplishments in the role prior to redundancy, and why you think these achievements gave you the necessary skills to be a great trainee solicitor.

Job-seeking is also a perfectly valid reason for a gap in your CV. Explain how you've been actively searching for the right role, and state that you've used the time to consider exactly what you hope to accomplish and the direction you want to take as a solicitor. If you've undertaken any courses or training while job-hunting, talk about them, or perhaps you've been doing some volunteer work – whatever it is, use it! You can then go on to explain why you think the role is such a good fit.

DOS AND DON'TS

DO:

Do – Switch your phone off. If this sounds like an obvious one to you, then great! But you'd be surprised by the reports from recruiters of candidates texting, taking calls and even checking Facebook *during* the interview! Just turn it off before you enter the building, and leave it off, until you're back outside and well away. Mobile phone 'addicts' are easy to spot, and the tendency can leave a poor impression on prospective employers. It may sound surprising, but even the receptionist may be asked to give their impressions of you, as you arrived and left – so it's best to treat everyone to a smile and always be attentive and courteous.

Do – Be yourself. The interviewer wants to see the real you, so that they can assess how well you'd fit in as a trainee. Be natural, as well as professional.

Do – Mind your language. There's no need to put on an act or speak more formally than you usually do, but be aware of over-using filler words such as 'like' ("*I was, like, in charge of like, the whole, like, group presentation*") or prefixing every answer with 'So...' ("*What are your hobbies?*" "*OK, so, I like snowboarding and base jumping.*") Many legal recruiters are of a generation that find this at best, baffling, and at worst, extremely irritating. Similarly, if you're replying to an email from a recruiter, thank them for their email, don't thank them for 'reaching out'. It's another example of a fairly modern term that's become something of a pet peeve for some employers. Slang words are a part of everyday vernacular, but are best avoided in a legal interview setting. Swear words are a definite no, obviously!

Do – Follow instructions. If you're asked to bring certain documents or information with you to the interview, or to prepare a short presentation, read the instructions carefully. Not doing so suggests that you won't manage to follow instructions in the job either.

Do – Wear a watch – even if you have to borrow one. It gives the impression of someone who cares about being punctual.

DON'T:

Don't – Speak negatively about your current or previous employer. If you left your last job under a cloud, or you simply can't stand your current workplace, focus instead on what you've learned. When asked about why you left or are leaving, stick to the positives: *"I've really enjoyed improving my admin skills as an office junior, but I feel that I'm ready to do more hands-on property work and want to move into a conveyancing role."* Or, *"I'm looking for a new challenge that will bring out my potential, and in my current job I feel I've progressed as far as I can within that role."*

Don't – Exaggerate, embellish or lie. There is zero tolerance for dishonesty in the legal profession. You *will* get found out.

Don't – Give short answers. Even if you're asked a closed question (a question that only requires a 'yes' or 'no' answer, e.g. 'Did you enjoy university?') it's best to expand on your answer and give some detail. Use the sample answers to prepare your own key statements, and use the interviewer's questions to work the things *you* want to say into the conversation.

Don't – Drink and interview! It may be tempting for soothing the nerves, but no. Never do this.

NOTES

NOTES

QUESTIONS TO ASK YOUR INTERVIEWER

Career experts always recommend that you have questions prepared to ask in a job interview. Often, when candidates are asked at the end of the interview, 'Is there anything you'd like to ask us?' they mumble something like, 'I think you've already covered everything, thanks'. But there's no reason not to have a good question ready to fire off. In fact, it's best to have a small bank of them, just in case the interviewer has been extremely thorough in their explanations of the job role and the company.

Don't ask about holidays, salary or benefits at this stage – there will be plenty of time for negotiation after they've decided to hire you! Ask questions about the role, the company, the people, or the clients.

Below are a few suggestions for great questions to ask your interviewer. Turn the tables on them – be bold!

What do you like most about working here?

Pay attention to the answer. If they start talking about what a great area, location, place to live and not about the company itself, that could be a red flag. Also note how long it takes them to reply. Do they have to think hard to come up with the good points? This is your opportunity to interview the company and decide whether you like the idea of working there.

What challenges has the company faced in recent years?

This will give you an idea of how the company operates, what sort of issues affect it and how the team handles them. This is a great question to ask because it allows you to follow up with specific questions about particular challenges the company has dealt with.

Why is the position open?

This is not always an appropriate question for a training contract, but if it's unusual for the company to take on a trainee, or if there are more trainee vacancies than in previous years, it can be a legitimate question. You could rephrase it as 'How many trainees do you recruit each year?' or 'How often do you take on new staff?'

If the company is expanding and more work is coming in than they can currently handle, great. If someone within the firm has been promoted, great. If the last few people 'didn't work out' or 'weren't a great fit' or 'decided to move on', that could potentially be a warning sign. Or it could simply mean they weren't a good fit – ask enough questions to get a feel for staff satisfaction. A very high turnover of staff in a law firm is fairly unusual in Britain.

Some good follow-up questions if you're unsure might be:

How long has everyone worked here?

How would your current team describe the working environment here?

Can you tell me a little about the people I'll be working directly with?

Do the staff socialise outside work?

How would you describe the management style here?

What sort of things will I be doing for CPD hours if I'm successful?

What sort of cases will I be working on initially? How much autonomy will I have?

How are appraisals conducted, and how often do they take place?

Will there be any opportunity to utilise my Urdu/French/Japanese?

A good way to ask a question, whilst gently reminding the interviewer of your unique selling points! This question isn't limited to language skills, of course. You could also ask about opportunities to use other abilities you may have, such as marketing or business development.

Does the company accommodate flexible, hybrid or remote working?

Be careful with this one. Law firms are heavily paper-file based, which can make remote working impractical, especially for smaller practices. The legal profession is one that's generally resisted the home-working trend more than most, so a potential employee who appears to want to work remotely may not be an appealing prospect for a more traditional office. It can also be difficult to adequately supervise a trainee solicitor remotely (although that's not to say it can't be done). Many firms utilise remote working technology very well, but it may be more politic to try to ascertain this information from the company website beforehand if possible, or from chatting informally to current trainees, e.g. at law fairs.

Earlier on, you mentioned the possibility of working abroad – can you tell me a bit more about that, please?

For 'working abroad' you can substitute anything that's come up during the interview, perhaps to do with training seat rotation, management structure, company social events, and so on. It shows that you've been absorbing information and that you're genuinely interested in a future at the company.

Ask about opportunities for progression if it seems appropriate. For a training contract this will probably already be fairly obvious, but it's reasonable to ask about scope and timescales for progression and development within the company.

What qualities do your current trainees have, that made them successful in their role?

This is a great question to ask early on, if possible, because you can then tailor your own answers to the specific skills and qualities the recruiter is looking out for. If you don't get chance to ask until the end of the interview, it's still worth dropping in because you can follow up with examples of how you demonstrate those particular traits.

When do you hope to make a decision by?

Everyone is impatient to hear the result of their interview, so this is a perfectly legitimate question – it manages your own expectations and also underlines your enthusiasm.

NOTES

AFTER THE INTERVIEW

Send a follow-up 'thank you' email the day after the interview. An example might be:

Dear Anita,

Thank you for your time yesterday. It was lovely to meet you and the team, and I was very impressed by my visit to Perfect Law. I enjoyed hearing more about the role, particularly the establishing of a new commercial property team.

I have had a few more thoughts this evening about promoting this new service in the local business community, which I hope to be able to put to you if I am successful. Some are based on ideas I implemented when setting up a new office for a previous employer, others are new and unique to a local law firm.

Thanks again for considering my application. I look forward to hearing from you later this month.

Kind regards,
Johan

If you are not offered the training contract, be gracious. The legal profession is a close-knit network and law firms talk to one another. Sadly, some candidates occasionally take rejection badly and send very rude emails to the recruiter. Not a good idea! Your name will be noted and you'll struggle to get another interview offer.

Instead, don't be afraid to solicit feedback, unless you're specifically told otherwise. Not only does this demonstrate mature handling of a disappointing situation, it reinforces your interest and may provide valuable advice for the next interview. Many candidates who didn't make it on their first application applied again the following year, having implemented the feedback from the interviewer, and landed a training contract the second time around. It's also possible that the successful applicant might not work out! So keep going, even if you don't quite get there on the first attempt. You're not alone!

 NOTES

STARTING YOUR NEW POSITION

On the first day, arrive early, smartly dressed, and greet people with a smile. Don't worry, everyone there had a first day at some point, without exception.

Network with other trainees, at the same firm or in online groups. Join your local law society.

Talk. Give feedback. If you're not happy about something, speak up. You'll be respected for doing so, more than if you stay quiet and never stand up and be heard.

It may turn out that it's not the right fit after all. It can happen. If it's really not right for you, secure another role before handing in your notice, and wherever possible leave on good terms. The legal profession is a small world. There's a lot to learn and you won't know it all immediately, but it will come. Ask for help. Ask questions. You're there to learn; that's why it's called a *training* contract.

Good luck in your legal journey. You've chosen a fascinating and rewarding profession, and I hope you enjoy every moment.

~ Eleanor Edwards

☆ INTERVIEW 1 ☆

FIRM:

INTERVIEW DATE: _____

TIME: _____

ADDRESS: _____

_____

_____

INTERVIEWER'S NAME: _____

CONTACT NUMBER: _____

CONTACT EMAIL: _____

FOLLOW UP EMAIL SENT? ☐ _____

FEEDBACK EMAIL RECEIVED? ☐ _____

OFFER? ☐ _____

_____

NOTES / REMINDERS:

★ INTERVIEW 2 ★

FIRM:

INTERVIEW DATE: _____

TIME: _____

ADDRESS: _____

_____

_____

INTERVIEWER'S NAME: _____

CONTACT NUMBER: _____

CONTACT EMAIL: _____

FOLLOW UP EMAIL SENT? ☐ _____

_____

FEEDBACK EMAIL RECEIVED? ☐ _____

_____

OFFER? ☐ _____

_____

_____

NOTES / REMINDERS:

★ INTERVIEW 3 ★

FIRM:

INTERVIEW DATE:

TIME:

ADDRESS:

INTERVIEWER'S NAME:

CONTACT NUMBER:

CONTACT EMAIL:

FOLLOW UP EMAIL SENT? ☐

FEEDBACK EMAIL RECEIVED? ☐

OFFER? ☐

NOTES / REMINDERS:

★ INTERVIEW 4 ★

FIRM:

INTERVIEW DATE: _____

TIME: _____

ADDRESS: _____

_____

_____

INTERVIEWER'S NAME: _____

CONTACT NUMBER: _____

CONTACT EMAIL: _____

FOLLOW UP EMAIL SENT? ☐ _____

_____

FEEDBACK EMAIL RECEIVED? ☐ _____

_____

OFFER? ☐ _____

_____

_____

NOTES / REMINDERS:

☆ INTERVIEW 5 ☆

FIRM:

INTERVIEW DATE: _____

TIME: _____

ADDRESS: _____

_____

_____

INTERVIEWER'S NAME: _____

CONTACT NUMBER: _____

CONTACT EMAIL: _____

FOLLOW UP EMAIL SENT? ☐ _____

_____

FEEDBACK EMAIL RECEIVED? ☐ _____

_____

OFFER? ☐ _____

_____

_____

NOTES / REMINDERS:

Printed in Great Britain
by Amazon

37692595R00116